Liberating Fat Bodies

Wesley R. Bishop • Bessie N. Rigakos

Liberating Fat Bodies

Social Media Censorship and Body Size Activism

Wesley R. Bishop
Jacksonville State University
Jacksonville, AL, USA

Bessie N. Rigakos
Marian University
Indianapolis, IN, USA

ISBN 978-3-031-63889-3   ISBN 978-3-031-63890-9   (eBook)
https://doi.org/10.1007/978-3-031-63890-9

This Palgrave Macmillan imprint is published by the registered company Springer Nature Switzerland AG.
The registered company address is: Gewerbestrasse 11, 6330 Cham, Switzerland

Paper in this product is recyclable.

We Removed Something You Posted

Jon Hanna

We Removed Something You Posted
Your tone was strident. Your pain was raw.
It disturbed people we prefer comfortable.
We Removed Something You Posted
You showed your body. Your own body.
You were happy with it. You shouldn't be.
You were unhappy with it. Then hide it.
We Removed Something You Posted
A breast not beside a product.
A breast not made into a product.
That's obscene.
We Removed Something You Posted
Your face after you were beaten.
Your heart after you were raped.
That's violent.
We've reviewed the post that said they want you dead.
We've reviewed the post that said you should be raped.
If only you weren't too ugly to rape.
We've reviewed the sexual imagery you never asked for.
We've reviewed the mocking of your murdered brothers and sisters.
This did not violate our community standards.
How did you find this experience?
June 16, 2016

ACKNOWLEDGMENTS

This book owes its existence to many people, far too many to thank by name. However, some of the biggest supporters of this book deserve special thanks, for without them this entry into the field of fat studies would not have been possible.

First, we would like to thank the participants. We interviewed over a dozen individuals for this book. Although we completed many of the interviews in 2019 before the COVID pandemic, there were still a number we had to do through Zoom as closures and restrictions on travel became part of everyday life. As such, we are grateful that so many people took the time during a global health crisis to talk to us. In particular, we would like to thank Carina Shero who originally sat for an interview with Wes Bishop in 2018 for *TERSE*. From that interview the idea for this book was born. In November 2019, Carina opened her home and studio in Chicago for us to do the majority of the interviews. Alessandra Grima, Robina Strowder, Jessie Oliver, Vivienne Rose, and Carina made themselves available for multiple follow-up interviews, questions of clarification, and academic panels to discuss chapters of the book as we wrote them. Also, we thank Annie Brown, Asstyn Martin, Danielle Whitfield, Iridessence/Essence Walker, Grey Johnson, Jackie Barthelemy, Laura Weetzie Wilson, Phaedra Black, Dimple Duchess, Val Elefante, Jesse Duquette, and Audrey Grison.

This book is as much their endeavor as it is ours.

We also owe a large thanks to the editors at Palgrave Macmillan. They were incredibly patient with us as we worked on the manuscript, and extended our deadline several times as we went over pages, transcripts, and secondary literature. Writing a book is no small task, and given most of this was done during COVID, we particularly appreciate the editors' time and understanding.

Our colleagues at Marian University and Jacksonville State University, along with our students, also are owed thanks. In particular, Deeb Kitchen, Michelle Meer, Paul Beezley, Ryan Burns, Lindsay Holman, Alzbeta Hajkova, Jennifer Gross, Bri Turgeon, and Jenna Ridlen have been sources of support, allowing us to bounce ideas off of them, and opening their classes for us to come and discuss the book as we worked on the manuscript. We hope this continues after the publication, so that body size activism is better understood by students.

Ricardo Quintana-Vallejo and Cynthia Gwyne Yaudes offered edits and extensive feedback on the book in various stages, to which we are grateful. *The Southern Humanities Council, Labor and Working Class History Association, Appalachian Studies Association*, and *Radical Philosophy Association* also were huge sources of help as we presented drafts of the chapters at their academic meetings.

Special thanks also are felt to the late Jon Hanna and his wife Joanna Schaffalitzky. When we read Jon's poem early in the research for this book, we knew we wanted to include it. Joanna was kind enough to agree to let us reprint the poem. We hope this helps promote a gifted writer who was taken from us far too soon.

Finally, we owe thanks to our family members who supported us on this endeavor. To Nek and Ari, thank you. To Allison, thank you for always being willing to talk through ideas; your grasp of radical politics and self-love made this book much more insightful.

We dedicate this book to you.

CONTENTS

LIST OF FIGURES

CHAPTER 1

Introduction: Liberating Fat Bodies and Online Censorship

Abstract Online platforms such as Instagram, Twitter/X, etc. have engaged in harmful censorship against users on the basis of body size. This book looks at the testimonies of over a dozen individuals who are involved in either fat liberation or who have knowledge about the unfair user experiences and work conditions many people, particularly women, endure when they navigate social media. This section examines the meanings behind the term "body size activism" and offers specific definitions for the following—body positivity, fat liberation, and body neutrality. It establishes the methodology of the study, as well as gives the reader an overview of who specifically was interviewed and how the researchers found them for the book. This Introduction also discusses the origin of this study and provides definitions for types of censorship—such as "shadow banning"— and theoretical ideas of why anti-fatness happens in these spaces—white supremacy, corporate capitalism, and republican political economy.

Keywords Fat liberation • Body positivity • Body neutrality • Shadow banning • Republican political economy • Censorship • Social media

© The Author(s), under exclusive license to Springer Nature Switzerland AG 2024
W. R. Bishop, B. N. Rigakos, *Liberating Fat Bodies*,
https://doi.org/10.1007/978-3-031-63890-9_1

Alessandra Grima poses with cello. Such work is representative of the art fat models in the body size acceptance movement create to challenge anti-fat bias

Body size activism is a vital social movement. The movement to end discrimination based on body size dates back several decades, but in the early twenty-first century it has emerged as central to understanding how societal oppression operates. The movement to liberate fat bodies seeks to empower people of all body shapes and sizes, reject harmful cultural norms, and most importantly end the stigma of fatness.

This book grew out of a single interview with the German American activist, model, and artist Carina Shero, who has been repeatedly targeted by Instagram for allegedly violating its community guidelines. Her account, @unskinnyhero, had well over 400,000 followers before Instagram deleted it in 2018. That deletion was the eighth time Instagram had targeted Shero for outright banning or softer forms of censorship, sometimes called "shadow banning."

Shadow banning, also known as "stealth banning," is a practice social media platforms use to limit the visibility of certain users' content without notifying them. This means that the content remains visible to the user who posted, but is hidden from others, making it difficult to gain followers, maintain engagement, or spread any message.

"I had really hoped we had moved past this issue of fat phobia on Instagram," Shero stated. "But apparently the company is at the moment deleting pretty much every plus size Instagram model that is working in lingerie or just generally in the realm of sexy or seductive."[1] She explained that she was appearing in a film at the time and was expected to advertise it on her social media sites. "[T]he producers just called me yesterday and were like, 'Uh … hey we are really worried. What's going on with your account? Are you going to get it back?'" Shero continued, "This is my job. So, without my account I am currently jobless. I still have my Patreon and my other platforms, but Instagram has been my main hub to show my work, to get sponsors, and to guide people to my other sites. I've also spent the most time curating my presence on Instagram and so without that profile to lead people to places like my Patreon, I just don't have a job."[2]

For fat activists and artists like Carina Shero these types of censorship, outright or stealthy, are damaging, as they not only limit their ability to

[1] Wesley Bishop and Carina Shero "Instagram Deleted Her Account @ Over 400K Followers: Fat Phobia in Art and Social Media, and How Carina Shero Continues to Fight for Better Representation of All Bodies," *TERSE*, April 15, 2018. https://tersejournal. com/2018/04/19/instagram-deleted-her-account-over-400k-followers-fat-phobia-in-art-and-social-media-and-how-carina-shero-continues-to-fight-for-better-representation-of-all-bodies/.

[2] Ibid.

work but also create social media landscapes that are void of diversity. In attempts to raise awareness about body size activism, then, the message can become lost, or controlled by big tech companies that select who gets to speak and participate in the digital sphere. Unfortunately, as this book shows, this issue of censorship toward body size activism and its expressions online is not an isolated case. We hope that by providing this study we can document the history of an aspect of body size activism, analyze its impact, and celebrate the voices of some of those who have fought for its cause.

METHODOLOGY

The methodology used in this study is informed by a socio-historical perspective, which recognizes the importance of understanding how social, cultural, and historical contexts shape the experience and perspectives of the individual being studied. Seventeen individuals were interviewed, six of whom agreed to sit down for follow-up discussions. This allowed the study to gather information on shifting understandings of body size activism, the volatile nature of social media regulations, and how events like the George Floyd uprising, the January 6th insurrection, and the COVID-19 pandemic affected thinking.

Our sampling method was primarily a snowball sampling of chain referrals. The initial interviewees were supplied by Shero, who has created a network in Chicago and the upper Midwest. From there, the researchers branched out to include other fat users on social media, primarily focusing on fat women who were involved in body size activism or who were artists that social media sites targeted for censorship. Not all participants we contacted agreed to interview. In one case, Shero explained that there was a hesitancy that two academics would not treat the issue or the stories of the participants seriously. We acknowledge that this fear is both legitimate and unfortunate. The academy has not historically been a place to affirm voices of the marginalized, particularly regarding body size, the adult performance industry, or sex positivity. Our hope is that this book will at least demonstrate how academics can better relate to marginalized people in society, serving not as voyeur but as colleagues and advocates.

Of the participants, eleven identified as white, while six identified as people of color. Five of those participants identified as Black. Two of the participants identified as male. This included Grey Johnson, a photographer and Black artist who works with fat models and is often targeted for anti-fatness, racism, and misogyny, and Jesse Duquette, a cartoonist and white man who does not primarily work in body size activism but is involved in the anti-racist and general progressive movements of early twenty-first-century America.

Two other participants, Annie Brown and Val Elefante, are sex-positive activists and technologists who created a new digital space called Lips.com in response to censorship from platforms like Instagram. These four interviews are included as supporting information and insight into how artists who are not models have handled online censorship and how some have created specific spaces to try to combat this. Finally, we interviewed Audrey Grison, a French model, artist, and disability rights activist who uses social media for her work.

This study also provides standard definitions for the various aspects of body size activism, tools and methods of online censorship, and the concept of republican political economy. Also, as will be shown in subsequent chapters, the issue of body size activism and the public sphere (space, media, and conceptions of the public) have been part of body size activism since the earliest fat liberation groups.

Body Size Activism

Body size activism has a rich history that can be traced back to the early 1960s as a distinct movement separate from others. As Charlotte Cooper explains, "The concept of fat liberation emerged out of the radical political and cultural movements of the late 1960s and early 1970s."[3] In her book, *Fat Activism: A Radical Social Movement,* Cooper interviewed activists to create a historical timeline of fat liberation politics as well as providing clarification on several concepts such as the problems of using the word "obesity," why "body positivity" was neither fat liberation nor liberatory, and finally how knowledge about "health" and fat discrimination should be based on accounts and communities of those most negatively impacted by the medical industry. As she states:

> The study was originally proposed by my supervisors to the funding body as a piece of research about anti-fat discrimination in the dietetic clinic … The proposal reflected my supervisors' and the funders' interests more than mine

---

[3] Charlotte Cooper, *Fat Activism: A Radical Social Movement* (Bristol, Eng.: HammerOn Press, 2016), 1.

and did not consider the possible effect on a fat researcher ... A different approach was required that reflected my experience and knowledge of fat ... This change of focus transformed the work. Instead of research that reproduced fat people's helplessness and marginalization, which dwelt on fat hatred and abjection, or reinforced medical supremacy, or the power of the expert, or reiterated claims about anti-fat discrimination that are already well-worn and deeply known to fat people, I was free to explore the political imaginations of fat community. I could say something new.[4]

In the same vein, this book continues this work. Whereas Cooper traced the historical development of fat liberation from mid-twentieth-century US politics to the communities she interviewed in the United Kingdom, this book makes the same tracing but leads off into some of the online communities that developed in the 2010s. Although we discuss issues around the medical industrial complex, and health and diet industries, our study looks at how these heirs of the first wave of body size activism continued in online spaces and have had to wrestle with issues of social, economic, and political marginalization. Likewise, it demonstrates, as did Cooper, how the knowledge of being a fat person leads to different views on a host of topics.

An example of this difference in view was revealed to us almost immediately as we began the interviews in how different participants defined the social movement they were involved with. Although it has become something of a standard aside in the literature to begin with an explanation of why body positivity is not fat liberation, and why fat liberation is preferable, the term "body positivity" persists.[5]

While some participants believed the term "body positivity" encompassed all actions related to social justice and personal liberation concerning body size, others felt it was a whitewashed version of a more radical movement such as fat liberation.

"I know that that is debated," Vivienne Rose explained in one of her interviews. "Body positivity is [to me] celebrating yourself as you are, the thing you need, the things you require, the things you want, the things

---

[4] Ibid., 5.
[5] For an example of the criticism of body positivity and an endorsement for fat liberation specifically, see Aubrey Gordon, *What We Don't Talk About When We Talk About Fat* (Boston: Beacon Press, 2020), Charlotte Cooper, *Fat Activism: A Radical Social Movement* (Bristol, Eng.: HammerOn Press, 2016), Da'Shaun L. Harrison, *Belly of the Beast: The Politics of Anti-Fatness as Anti-Blackness*, (San Francisco: North Atlantic Books, 2021).

you desire. Loving you in everything that you are comprised of from head to toe."[6] (Fig. 1.1).

Other participants, however, reported that they felt that body positivity was simply the safer version of a more emancipatory movement. "When I first found out about body positivity," Saucye West stated, "I found out about it through [the] fat activism community, which is where body positivity was basically first from. When I was in a community with activists, I

Fig. 1.1 Vivienne Rose, a Texas-based model and activist in the fat activist movement, poses with a chair. Aside from creating images that show the beauty of fat bodies, another major concern fat activists point to is the lack of accessible seating in public spaces

[6] Vivienne Rose interview by Wesley R. Bishop, Indianapolis, Indiana, May 20, 2021.

started to do events … we would hear about the diversions of the body positive movement, which was being led of course by commissioned only size, white people."[7]

Essence Walker echoed this sentiment by stating, "I would say I don't have a total issue with body positivity … I think in a perfect world, it would be really great in the sense that everybody does have [body] issues. Whether or not they have socially acceptable bodies or not, everybody at some point will have some sort of self-esteem issue. [Body positivity] is helpful in that sense, but it does very little for the real persecution that people of size face as far as health industry woes, [and] job industry woes."[8] Walker continued with:

> I remember one thing that just blew my mind. I remember reading some years ago … that juries were literally less likely to trust larger defendants or plaintiffs … I was like, "Wow," It's really that bad that the jury will look at you and say … will think … subconsciously…, "You're fat. I don't trust you. You're probably greedy. You're probably bad.' … So things like body positivity, I don't really know [how] much they're going to help the fact that that happens, or doctors will take one look at you and misdiagnose you or not give you the proper care you need based on your size. Things like that, that I don't think body positivity really addresses.[9]

Therefore, there is a tension in how mainstream society has come to classify and use the terms body positivity and fat liberation. As participants stated throughout the interviews, fat liberation was a more social justice, anti-racist, and outward-focused movement that combatted anti-fat bias in the realms of civil and legal rights. Body positivity was more an inner liberation movement geared toward body acceptance and "decolonizing one's mind." Carina Shero, in a follow-up interview in 2022 acknowledged this tension and reflected that although the term "body positivity" was limited, it was, for better or worse, the term that had gained widespread traction. Perhaps, she thought, the term would just have to do when discussing both body positivity and fat liberation.

To this concern this project consciously uses the term "body size activism" as the umbrella term to encompass body positivity, fat liberation, and body neutrality as interrelated but differently focused aspects of a broader

---

[7] Saucye West Zoom interview by Wesley R. Bishop, Aug. 9, 2021.
[8] Essence Walker interview by Wesley R. Bishop, Chicago, Illinois, Nov. 4, 2019.
[9] Essence Walker also goes by Iridessence. She asked that we use both names in the book.

social movement. When referring to body positivity we therefore adhere to the more specified movement of personal psychological states, self-love, corporate campaigns, and acknowledge that body positivity is "for everyone" since it can include smaller-sized bodies that struggle with body image, eating disorders, etc.[10] When referring, though, to the specific movement that deals with discrimination against fat bodies in transportation, medicine, employment, and law, we will use the specific term "fat liberation." As we show in this work, fat liberation has a long history stretching through the civil rights, anti-racist, and anti-colonial movements.

During our research we became aware of a lesser-discussed aspect of body size activism—body neutrality. Body neutrality corresponds to both body positivity, in that it focuses on the thinking of individuals, but it differs in the idea that human bodies, be they fat, thin, disabled, etc., should be "celebrated." Instead, body neutrality argues that bodies should be seen, first, as integral to a human being, not separate, and therefore not be valued on any basis of aesthetics. In this way, body neutrality relates to fat liberation because it seeks a deconstruction of value placed on bodies, and a more equitable treatment of people, yet it differs in that fat liberation (as we found in our interviews) makes considerable space to not just fight for social justice but also to celebrate fatness in media depictions, erotica, and art. As Shero stated, "We are glorious and we should be able to move on from neutrality."[11] Yet when conversations in the interviews turned to medical professionals and government agencies mistreating fat people, there was a complete agreement that some form of equality needed to be achieved and that this equality should be based in part on impartiality to make moral judgements about different body sizes. Overall, while there are tensions in how society has come to classify and use terms such as body positivity and fat liberation, we believe that using the term "body size activism" allows for a more nuanced and inclusive discussion of the various movements within the larger movement. We also acknowledge that achieving equality for people of all body sizes requires impartiality in making moral judgments about different body sizes.

---

[10] The exception to this will be when participants use "body positivity" in their interviews or when secondary sources conflate body positivity with either fat liberation or body size activism.

[11] Carina Shero interview by Wesley R. Bishop, Chicago, Illinois, April 14, 2022.

Online Censorship

Online censorship is a growing concern in the digital age, as platforms are increasingly using algorithms to regulate and control the flow of information. One form of censorship that has garnered attention in recent years is shadow banning. Before we can progress further, it is helpful to define these two terms—shadow banning and algorithms. For the purposes of this research, we define shadow banning as the act of selectively hiding or suppressing content or accounts on social media platforms without notifying the affected users. This can be done by reducing the visibility of posts or accounts, limiting the reach of certain content, or making it more difficult to find.

Algorithms are often used to implement shadow banning, as they are capable of automatically flagging and filtering content that is deemed inappropriate or in violation of platform policies. These algorithms use a variety of signals and criteria to determine what content should be suppressed or promoted, including keywords, user behavior, and engagement metrics.

In subsequent chapters we will look at "softer" forms of online censorship such as bullying, harassment, targeted campaigns, misuse of hashtags, and familial and work pressures to not appear as fat and celebratory in online spaces. The two discussed here are simply two of the least understood ways social media sites discriminate and censor fat folks, people of color, and people with disabilities.

The first of these terms, "shadow banning," refers to how online platforms have found ways to censor users without completely doing so. What this means is that instead of deleting an account (which does frequently happen for users on sites such as Instagram and TikTok), the platform will effectively soft censor users, hoping to decrease their influence, their ability to reach other members of the platform's community, and eventually drive them into irrelevance or frustration to quit the platform altogether. Interviewees reported such practices as not appearing in search functions for particular periods (something we discovered during this research), being unable to use hashtags or specific hashtags (thereby limiting their reach) and created content suddenly dropping in popularity. Interviewees noted that they would notice posts of theirs that typically would have thousands of likes and engagement would suddenly drop to the hundreds overnight. Worse was the fact that this soft censorship (the content was permitted to be posted but would not appear in feeds) felt like gaslighting.

There was no official proof that the user was being targeted for censorship. This leaves folks questioning if there is discrimination or simply that their content was not "good." This gaslighting can be seen in the more formal reporting on social media as Elaine Moore at the *Financial Times* illustrated:

> [S]ocial media influencers are at the mercy of algorithms. This makes them perfect fodder for conspiracy theories. It also makes sense that influencers would be baffled by any sudden decrease in engagement and spooked by changes that might jeopardise the brand deals they sign. Instead of believing that their own popularity is waning, some cling to the idea that shadowbans are a disciplinary measure that is used against creators who do not warrant an outright ban from a platform.[12]

Moore's comments demonstrate that fat users therefore must deal with the twin issues of censorship and formal outlets not believing them. Is the discrimination they are facing real? Or is it just imagined? Is there an anti-fat bias, or is it just that the content is unappealing to the public? Interviewees reported that this aspect of the censorship was particularly hard because it affected mental health in previously unexpected ways.

Moore's analysis, however, does lead to the next tool of online censorship—algorithms. Algorithms in computer science simply mean a set of rules or procedures where, in this case computers, use calculations or other problem-solving operations to follow and determine functions.[13] This means that technically algorithms can refer to a host of computer technology and practices, but when users and members of online body size activism groups use it they mean specifically the practice that social media companies use to push particular content at the cost of lower visibility for other content. This often relates to a kind of pay-for-view approach to social media sites that will favor big corporate brands or higher-paying users to get their message to users at the expense of the more organic and community-based visibility that social media initially promised.

At this juncture it appears that many of these issues of anti-fat bias have a decidedly capitalist bent. Social media companies' desires to generate

---

[12] Elaine Moore, "The Truth about 'Shadowbanning' Is More Complicated than Influencers Think," *Financial Times*, March 12, 2022. Accessed January 3, 2023. https://www.ft.com/content/532d7a85-33c8-4488-a57d-9b226c77417a.

[13] Cathy O'Neil, *Weapons of Math Destruction: How Big Data Increases Inequality and Threatens Democracy* (New York: Crown, 2016).

more profit leads them to engage in practices that favor more economically powerful entities while punishing users who have no economic clout. Although that is undeniably a factor in this, it is not the only issue, and, as we argue, it is far from the biggest barrier to body size activism online. As online platforms continue to play a prominent role in public discourse, our goal is to ensure that these platforms are transparent and accountable in their moderation practices, and that users can express themselves freely without fear of censorship or suppression.

REPUBLICANISM NOT NEOLIBERALISM

Although capitalism provides a system of exploitation and oppression, it is not the neoliberal form of capitalism that many fat activists have had to contend with in terms of discrimination in the ability to represent online fat bodies. Instead, it is an older form of political economy, republican capitalism, where idealized forms of democracy and citizen limit what we as a society are willing to view as legitimate modes of human existence.

Capitalism as a political economy is not the sole source of anti-fat bias in our society. In fact, it could be more than possible to obtain many of the goals of some of the body size activists' movements (in particular, body positivity) while maintaining capitalism. Likewise, socialism can (and has) easily adopted anti-fat language and images in its own movements. The diet industry and beauty industry do use anti-fat bias to sell products, but they could just as easily use aspects of body size activism to create and market new commodities. When interviewees were asked about this tension, and why, if fat people as both models and consumers could generate more revenue for corporations, they openly admitted that "fat sells." Participants stated they believed the censorship was less over loss of profit, and more an issue of "morality police" where "good" and "bad" are enforced to create idealized communities of only certain images and people. To simply allow some nude images, like the accounts of the Kardashians, Gwyneth Paltrow, *Playboy*, while banning sex workers and models of OnlyFans and the site PornHub is, to rework the line of the poet Maggie Nelson, "puritanism not pornography."[14]

---

[14] Maggie Nelson specifically calls this "eros" and chastises men who want to see naked women, but minus any perceived imperfection. "What good is my peek at her pubic hair if I must also see the red lines made by her panties, the pimples on her rump, broken veins like

Republican capitalist political economy values "fitness" and certain body types as the ideal for its citizens. Any deviation from that becomes a threat to a supposed "free society." This leads to a situation where fat activists and artists are routinely hounded to conceal their bodies and their message that we, as a society, need to stop discrimination based on body size. The body size activism approach of using platforms to share images that challenges the traditional aesthetic does require a public. It requires that others view fat bodies first as not problems to be fixed, but then beyond that as not just a thing of beauty and fetishization. The body size activism approach of using images requires the viewer to see fat bodies as a person, embodied in a corporeal body. Fat liberation leads us to collapse the body-mind duality, forcing us to see the fat body as an expression of lived human experience, deserving dignity, respect, and rights. Yet that only happens with a public. Without someone to see the act of fat and human life, then the act of taking a selfie, unapologetically fat, becomes a private affair. It may help us individually, but it does not help as much with the collective issues surrounding fat discrimination. As such, the censorship of fat bodies on social media sites is an attack not just on the person being censored, nor just one movement, but instead it is an admission of an entire system of bigotry that denies a whole group of humanity access to shared public commons. It is the further denial of basic civil rights for a whole group of humans.

Conclusion

This book explores the rich history and current landscape of body size activism, with a particular focus on the role of social media in this movement. Through examining the backgrounds of participants, the impact of traditional media, and the need for a public to fully embrace the goals of body size activism, we will share a deeper understanding of the challenges and opportunities facing this movement. While also considering the broader implications of social media for activism, including its potential to both support and hinder progress.

This book is organized into five different thematic chapters that delve into different aspects of body size activism. Chapter 2 looks at the way that social media users, specifically fat women, have used the ability to post

the print of a lavender thumb, the stepped-on look of a day's-end muff? I've that at home. ... This is puritanism, not eros." See Maggie Nelson, *Bluets* (New York: Wave Books, 2009), 24.

pictures of themselves to both challenge societal conceptions of fatness and work through personal perception they and their family have concerning anti-fat bias. It examines how some of these women have turned their online personas into both artistic and business ventures, and the frequent harassment they face for being fat women online. Chapter 3 focuses on the differences and similarities between social media and traditional forms of media. It looks at how participants in this study view the issue of body positivity co-optation by both corporations and thin-to-average-size white women. It also questions developments in the body neutrality movement. Chapter 4 examines the intersection of fatness and the public sphere, exploring the need for a public to fully realize the aims of body size activism. It also delves more deeply into the concept of republican political economy and how it reinforces anti-fat bias, ableism, and racism in society. Chapter 5 takes a closer look at social media, considering how it has been both a tool and a hindrance to the body size activism movement. Finally, Chap. 6 concludes with a look at the recent Supreme Court case in the summer of 2023, and the "26 Words that Created the Internet," which serves as a reminder of the immense power of the Internet and the urgent need for ongoing dialogue and advocacy to ensure that this power is harnessed for positive social change. By continuing to raise awareness and challenge harmful biases, we can work toward a world where body diversity is celebrated, and all individuals are valued for their unique contributions.

CHAPTER 2

Working While Fat in the Age of the Internet

Abstract This chapter examines how media users who are fat women have used the ability to post pictures of themselves to both challenge societal conceptions of fatness, as well as work through personal perception they and their family have concerning anti-fat bias. It examines how some of these women have turned their online personas into both artistic and business ventures, and the frequent harassment they face for being fat women online. The participants argued that despite the threats to losing other jobs for posting revealing photos, receiving unwanted advances and comments from men, and the problems that came from family seeing their photos, they—as fat women using social media—are willing to endure this to develop healthier relationships with their own bodies, advocate for fat liberation, and possibly make money as models, performers, and artists.

Keywords Online work • Gamergate • Self-expression • Online harassment • Instagram • Meta • Community Guidelines

© The Author(s), under exclusive license to Springer Nature
Switzerland AG 2024
W. R. Bishop, B. N. Rigakos, *Liberating Fat Bodies*,
https://doi.org/10.1007/978-3-031-63890-9_2

Essence Walker (Iridessence) is an anti-racist and fat liberation activist currently based in New Orleans. Her work explores the issues of race, beauty, body size, and historical dress and setting

INTRODUCTION

An authoritative and comprehensive history of the Internet has yet to be penned, but its transformative power on politics, economics, and culture is increasingly evident. Over the first two decades of the twenty-first century, the world witnessed a revolution in terms of politics, economics, and culture from as material migrated from traditional media to a digital sphere. This massive change included incorporating for the first time massive global participation of audiences to not only view and interact with media, but also generate their own content. This blurred the lines of private and public ownership of content, especially as social media became dominated by a few corporations and included users from around the planet. The Internet, by the 2020s, had become an amalgamation of political activism, cultural production, and economic activity.

As this digital landscape unfolded, it became apparent that the consequences of online actions were not confined within the bounds of cyberspace. There were clear signs that the world was moving in this direction, and that what happened "in the Internet" did not stay "there." The Y2K scare at the turn of the twentieth century exposed the potential havoc that information coded and stored in digital spaces could wreak on national and global economies. According to sociologist Zeynep Tufekci, by 2016, with revelations surrounding the sale of personal information by companies such as Facebook and the unauthorized access to voter data, the true scope of the digital realm only began to become apparent to members of the US federal government.[1]

Carina Shero argued that this lack of understanding of the Internet, social media sites, and newer forms of technology is apparent in listening to members of Congress try to explain technology or even begin approaching regulation.[2] Members of Congress often struggled to grasp the intricacies of these platforms, leaving them ill-equipped to regulate or address the growing power of social media and tech companies.[3] Notable

---

[1] Zeynep Tufekci, *Twitter and Tear Gas: The Power and Fragility of Networked Protest* (New Haven: Yale University Press, 2018).

[2] Carina Shero interview by Wesley R. Bishop, Chicago, Illinois, Nov. 4, 2019.

[3] Tarleton Gillespie, *Custodians of the Internet: Platforms, Content Moderation, and the Hidden Decisions that Shape Social Media* (New Haven: Yale University Press, 2021).

exceptions such as Donald Trump and Alexandria Ocasio-Cortez, who possessed a deeper understanding of these platforms, were able to deftly navigate the digital landscape, and effectively run circles around their counterparts who in the early twenty-first century showed little interest or ability to master the new technology or reign in the growing power of social media and tech companies.

This ignorance and alignment with big tech present troubling concerns for denizens of the Internet as labor laws, harassment protections, and civil rights often erode when individuals log on to work online. Labor laws and worker's protections are tenuous at best as they often are even in physical spaces. In other words, such protections, already precarious in physical spaces, become even more fragile within the digital realm.[4] Writer and cultural critic Lindy West describes this issue, where specifically women are targeted for online harassment and violence, as the "violent theft of time."[5] West firmly asserts the significance of these concerns, countering dismissals that reduce the issue to mere Internet-related problems. She emphasizes, "It … matters. [The harassment] is costing me time, potential income, and mental health. If you consider Twitter part of my work, which I do, it is tampering with a journalist's email to coerce them into pulling a story. It is, I think, illegal."[6]

Perhaps one of the most notorious cases illustrating these challenges is the Gamergate scandal. From August 2014 through 2015, politically motivated misogynists embarked on a multifaceted campaign to target and silence women in the video game industry, including video game designers and cultural critics. These wings of the online misogynist community were enraged that feminist media critics, such as Anita Sarkeesian, and video game designers, such as Zoë Quinn and Brianna Wu, were part of a concerted effort to make video games and video gaming culture less sexist and violent toward women. Misogynists repeatedly doxed, threated to rape

---

[4]Catherine Buni and Soraya Chemaly, "The Unsafety Net: How Social Media Turned Against Women," *Atlantic*, Oct. 9, 2014. Accessed on December 21, 2023. https://www.theatlantic.com/technology/archive/2014/10/the-unsafety-net-how-social-media-turned-against-women/381261/.

[5]Lindy West, *Shrill: Notes from a Loud Woman* (New York: Hachette Books, 2016).

[6]West, *Shrill*, 109.

and murder, and demanded Sarkeesian, Quinn, and Wu end their criticisms of the gaming community.[7]

As we delve deeper into this chapter, we explore the experiences of individuals who face similar issues of online harassment while creating art, building businesses, and participating in the digital community on social media platforms. For instance, the participants we talked to reported very similar issues with online harassment as they created art, developed their businesses online, and engaged the larger digital community on social media platforms. In this chapter we will examine the intersection of this harassment with forms of censorship that arise not only from big tech companies but also from other users, family members, friends, and workplaces. Additionally, the outcome of the comments and targeted campaigns from other users, comments and concerns from family, friends, and places of work, and the toll these had on mental health have to be taken into consideration when assessing how the Internet in the period of social media has affected both users and broader social movements, such as body size activism.

REACTIONS FROM FAMILY, FRIENDS, AND WORK

Alessandra Grima, a New England–based artist and stand-up comedian, recalled a pivotal moment on Instagram that had a profound impact on her self-acceptance journey. She remembered the nerve-wracking experience of posting a picture of a bra she had purchased, without even revealing her face. This seemingly simple act stirred up intense emotions, leading to strained relationships with some of her family members, even to this day.

> The first post I did that gave me a heart attack was of just a bra that I bought. And it was just a bra and not even my face. I was shaking posting it and I lost family members posting that to this day.[8]

At that time, encountering individuals with diverse body types on Instagram was still relatively uncommon, unlike today. This revelation was a turning point for Grima, prompting her to embark on a path of self-acceptance and explore the possibilities of utilizing social media platforms

---

[7] Torill Elvira Mortensen, "Anger, Fear, and Games: The Long Event of #GamerGate," *Games and Culture* 13:8 (2018), 787–806.

[8] Alessandra Grima, Zoom interview by Wesley R. Bishop, May 15, 2023.

to establish small businesses. These ventures included comedy, tarot readings, and different forms of adult entertainment and modeling.

Grima's journey began shortly after losing her job, when she still remembers lacking self-esteem, a feeling she had well into her late twenties. Her confidence started to grow, though, after receiving positive feedback for some headshots she had taken for acting purposes. It was during this period that she discovered the presence of fat individuals on Instagram, which was a groundbreaking realization for her. Back then, seeing someone with a larger body size on social media was a novelty. This discovery played a significant role in shaping Grima's aspirations and motivating her to create her own small businesses.

> I really had no self-esteem until probably my late twenties ... So, I started my Instagram coming out of feeling kind of good about headshots [I had gotten for acting]. And I started following or noticing that there were fat people on Instagram, which sounds normal today, but ten years ago that was big ... Just seeing someone fat on Instagram ... I've never seen that before in my life.[9]

Grima, like many Instagram artists and performers, relies on social media sites in the digital economy, such as OnlyFans and Patreon, to promote her work, engage with her audience, and direct them to such platforms. These social media platforms, then, are crucial tools for artists such as Grima to showcase their talents and connect with their fans.

Similarly, Saucye West, a model and activist, shared her experience of her family's gradual transformation in their attitude toward her online presence. Despite enduring trauma in her younger years, West chose to assert herself and push past the negative perceptions imposed on her. As time passed, her family embraced a more accepting and supportive stance toward her work and social movement campaigns, recognizing the significance of her endeavors. "With my family, they've been dealing with it for a long time. They know how I am. They['re] not worried about me. Back in the day it was different because ... [my family was] ... where a lot of my trauma came from [when] I was younger ... When I had my light switch moment, which was at the age of fourteen ... [I decided] you're not going

---

[9] Ibid.

to talk about me like that anymore. I'm not going to have it. You guys did enough damage. So, I was like, let's move forward."[10]

Jackie Barthelemy, a social media user and burlesque performer, shared her thoughts on the complex emotions associated with posting pictures of her body online. In her experience, being raised in a traditional Mexican household initially sparked concerns about her mother's potential reaction. However, through sharing her clothing choices and participating in burlesque, Barthelemy opened dialogues within her family about fat acceptance and body positivity, ultimately fostering a more supportive and understanding dynamic.

> I think the biggest thing I was worried about was probably my mom. I come from a very Mexican traditional household. So, my mom started noticing my clothes were getting a little tighter. I was wearing the crop tops, so she was just like, 'Your shirts up.' I'm like, 'It's supposed to be.' So, it took her a while. We've had lots of conversations and stuff like that and I'm just like … she's plus size herself. And it's been … she's gotten better.[11]

Barthelemy explained that by posting the photos of herself, wearing clothing that she wanted, and by moving into performing burlesque although negative comments did come from her family it was a place to begin discussions about fat acceptance and more generalized body positivity:

> And so, I've gotten [comments that are] like, "Oh my God, I love seeing you wear clothes, and your body looks like mine." And it's just been really good … you usually see hourglass figure women, flat stomachs, stuff like that. And so, it's nice to just represent like, oh this is the other spectrum, we're out here too with this body shape … [my mom has] gotten better … Before … when I was younger and up until she saw that I was taking [fat acceptance] really seriously, she was very judgmental about my body. There was lots of pinching and my shirt being [tugged] down and stuff like that. But I think that she knows I'm at a place right now, where I'm just like, I want to be comfortable in my body at whatever size it was. Because I was smaller when I was younger and you look back at pictures and you're like, oh, I thought I was so big, and I wasn't that big. And I was that uncomfortable with my body, so I just want to be comfortable at whatever size I am. But my mom has been very supportive, now that she knows that I just don't

[10] West Zoom interviewed by Wesley R. Bishop, Aug. 9, 2021.
[11] Jackie Barthelemy interview by Wesley R. Bishop, Chicago, Illinois, Nov. 1, 2019.

care anymore … She's definitely come around. She supports me in … the whole burlesque thing, she likes it. She's seen my pictures and my videos. She's going to come to my show for the first-time next month. So, it's exciting. So, I'm glad she finally came around.[12]

This transformative process aligns with the scholarly works of Lisa Nakamura and Sarah Banet-Weiser, who shed light on the ways in which individuals challenge societal norms and navigate online spaces. Lisa Nakamura's research delves into the intersections of race, gender, and technology, emphasizing the importance of representation and agency for marginalized individuals. Her work highlights how digital platforms can be spaces for self-expression and activism, enabling individuals such as Barthelemy to challenge cultural expectations and promote body positivity.[13]

Similarly, Sarah Banet-Weiser explores the relationship between popular culture, media, and femininity. Her insights emphasize the significance of media consumption and production in shaping identity and challenging conventional notions of beauty. Banet-Weiser's work provides a framework for understanding Barthelemy's journey as she utilized social media and burlesque to engage her family in discussions about fat acceptance and body positivity.[14]

Through the lenses of Nakamura and Banet-Weiser, Barthelemy's story exemplifies the transformative power of online platforms and cultural expression in fostering supportive dynamics within families. The ability to use online platforms, then, to control how their bodies looked—clothed or nude—is an aspect of social media use participants agreed was a significant factor in combatting their own senses of insecurity, anti-fat bias, and develop a healthier and happier relationship with themselves.

Asstyn Martin, a model and adult performer, recounted how her journey into the adult industry became a source of empowerment. After leaving an abusive relationship, Martin discovered the beauty of diversity through receiving positive feedback about her body. Despite encountering negativity, the overwhelming support she received far outweighed the

---

[12] Ibid.

[13] Lisa Nakamura, *Digitizing Race: Visual Cultures of the Internet* (Minnesota: University of Minnesota Press, 2007).

[14] Sarah Banet-Weiser, *Empowered: Popular Feminism and Popular Misogyny* (Durham: Duke University Press, 2018).

criticism. This validation and encouragement from her audience further solidified her journey of self-acceptance and empowerment:

> Well, it really started for me, after I got out of an abusive relationship and started dating and started getting more positive feedback about my body as it was. And when I decided to get into the adult industry, that really actually helped me. It was very liberating to be able to take my clothes off, present myself as I was, and to hear all kinds of positive things. Which of course, there are always going to be negatives, but the positives far outweigh the negatives for me. And it helped me to realize, the world would be a pretty boring place if we all looked alike. And that maybe I shouldn't be so rough on myself.[15]

The ability to control their body representations, clothed or nude, on online platforms allows participants to combat insecurities, challenge anti-fat biases, and develop healthier relationships with themselves. Grima acknowledges the importance of not letting concerns about family judgments hinder financial success and personal happiness. "I realized that I look the ugliest in here," Grima said gesturing to her head. "So, seeing [the photos] in front of my face, I'm like, 'Oh, that wasn't so bad' … but I don't need crazy aunty. You know what I mean? I'd rather be happy and not have to deal with my asshole cousin … getting over what people think [of you and what you do] is where I started making money. I tell people that all the time. I'm like, 'if you care about what your family's going to find out, you're not going to make any money.'"[16]

The experiences of family pushback and fear of how acquaintances would treat them for either engaging in body size activism online or using their bodies as employment in adult entertainment and/or modeling constitutes a softer form of censorship, which is not new for fat people. Yet the participants in this study consistently stated that they were able to swiftly overcome these challenges or use their work as a catalyst for important conversations with their loved ones. It is important to note that this study focuses on individuals who actively continue to use social media in these ways, as those who conform to societal norms dictated by employers or family members may not engage in such work at all. Nevertheless, the work of the participants and other fat social media users plays a crucial role in countering the limited portrayals of human bodies in the media. By

[15] Asstyn Martin Zoom interview by Wesley R. Bishop, June 24, 2021.
[16] Alessandra Grima Zoom interview by Wesley R. Bishop, via Zoom call, May 15, 2023.

challenging societal norms and representing diverse bodies, they frame fat bodies as sexy, desirable, and beautiful, promoting acceptance and desirability.[17]

In contrast, the next form of soft censorship that will be explored is online harassment, which manifests in a far more explicit and violent manner. This form of censorship exposes the profound failure of social media sites in providing a safe working environment.[18] Within the realm of online harassment, the breakdown in workplace safety becomes evident, highlighting the consistent inability of social media platforms to adequately protect their users from harassment and abuse.

ONLINE HARASSMENT

Founded in 2010, Instagram was from its earliest iterations primarily a photo-sharing site.[19] In the following years, it became embroiled in debates over online censorship of diverse bodies, permittance of hate speech, and negative effects on young teenagers.[20] Ironically, Instagram's CEO Kevin Systrom had initially bragged about the site as a space committed to a kinder, gentler internet. "I've seen how other companies have misstepped in managing communities. People say Instagram is super positive and optimistic. In fact, we have a ton of negative stuff, but we're going after it before we have a problem."[21]

Systrom touted the platform as a "Technology of Kindness," and claimed that as a company they would go after negative content proactively. He believed, that Instagram unlike Twitter, Facebook, and YouTube was better in terms of providing safe and nurturing environments. The

---

[17] Melissa Gregg, *Counterproductive: Time Management in the Knowledge Economy* (Durham: Duke University Press, 2018). Angela McRobbie, *The Aftermath of Feminism: Gender, Culture and Social Change* (Los Angeles: SAGE Publications, 2009). Sarah Banet-Weiser, *The Most Beautiful Girl in the World: Beauty Pageants and National Identity* (Berkeley: University of California Press, 1999).

[18] Sarah T. Roberts, *Behind the Screen: Content Moderation in the Shadows of Social Media* (New Haven: Yale University Press, 2021).

[19] Todd Spangler, "Instagram CEO Positions His Company as Safer Alternative to Controversial Rivals," *Variety*, Nov .15, 2017. Accessed February 13, 2023. https://variety.com/2017/digital/features/instagram-ceo-kevin-systrom-1202614763/.

[20] Whitney Phillips, *This Is Why We Can't Have Nice Things: Mapping the Relationship between Online Trolling and Mainstream Culture* (Cambridge: MIT Press, 2016).

[21] Spangler, "Instagram CEO Positions His Company as Safer Alternative to Controversial Rivals."

basic premise was that Instagram took a far more censoring and controlling role in what and how users could post on its platform. Hashtags were monitored, words automatically flagged as "undesirable" and "unsafe, and a culture of constant monitoring promoted that made users think before they did anything on the site. Despite these promises, controversies quickly arose regarding Instagram's negative impact on young girl's body image.[22] This paradox highlights Instagram's inconsistent approach to censorship, where it claims to promote safety while tolerating hate speech and harassment.

"If you're the one guy who is going to be mean in a list of comments, you feel totally out of place," he says. "We're trying to remove the bottom 1% of really awful stuff," Systrom bragged.[23] Yet despite the self-congratulations, Instagram would by 2021 be embroiled in a national controversy over their app's negative impact on young girls' body image. Much of this had to do with the top-down curated approach that Instagram increasingly favored, particularly after it was bought by Facebook in 2012. This aspect of censorship, formal and hard, will be explored in the next chapter, but it is important to note that from the outset Instagram positioned itself as different from the libertarian spaces of Facebook, YouTube, and Twitter, arguing that their ability to control content led to safer, happier user experiences.

What made this ironic is that many of the participants in our study directly challenged Instagram's continual tolerance of hate speech, white supremacy, sexual harassment, and other reactionary movements, while aggressively censoring fat people, disabled people, and people of color who chose to explore more explicit aspects of their sexuality. Despite reports of illegal behavior such as death threats and harassment, social

---

[22] Billy Perrigo, "Instagram Makes Teen Girls Hate Themselves. Is that a Bug or Feature?" *Time*, Sept. 16, 2021. Accessed February 15, 2023. https://time.com/6098771/instagram-body-image-teen-girls/. The Learning Network, "What Students Are Saying About How Social Media Affects Their Body Image," *New York Times*, March 31, 2022. Accessed February 15, 2023. https://www.nytimes.com/2022/03/31/learning/what-students-are-saying-about-how-social-media-affects-their-body-image.html. Dan Milmo and Clea Skopeliti, "Teenage girls, Body Image and Instagram's 'Perfect Storm,'" *Guardian*, Sept. 18, 2021. Accessed February 15, 2023. https://www.theguardian.com/technology/2021/sep/18/teenage-girls-body-image-and-instagrams-perfect-storm.

[23] Spangler, "Instagram CEO Positions His Company as Safer Alternative to Controversial Rivals."

media companies, including Instagram, often fail to respond effectively.[24] The platform's inaction and selective enforcement raise questions about the biases and identities of the CEOs and programmers who shape these policies. For instance, participants noted, Instagram and many other social media sites will typically fall back on the excuse that there is simply nothing they can do to prevent groups such as neo-Nazis from using their sites. "I was going to say it's interesting how Instagram keeps saying it's impossible for us to get rid of hate speech because a lot of the Nazi groups kept coming up and it's impossible for us to track those people down," Grima argued. "And I'm like, 'Well, you can track the #BBW [big beautiful women] pretty fucking easily. So how about we kind of maybe do that with other words' … It's absolute crap to me. You can't find hate speech, but you can find my fat ass in a bikini and delete it? Get your shit together. It's 2022."[25]

"I did report a death threat and [Instagram] didn't do anything about it," Asstyn Martin recounted. "Yeah, I mean, I had somebody in my DMs threatening me and he's done it to other people that I know as well." Yet despite having proof of this illegal behavior Instagram and other social media companies rarely respond in any kind of helpful manner, permitting the harassment to continue. "I've reported things that I found to be transphobic, antisemitic, racist, xenophobic, … and nothing was done. And I'm thinking, 'How is it that people can post that sort of thing, but find lingerie … offensive? It just doesn't seem right.'"[26]

To test these claims, we as authors used the reporting features on Instagram. Finding explicitly transphobic content that violated Instagram's stated community guidelines, we reported several posts in April 2023. These images ranged from memes that said transphobic remarks such as: "Him: I had my dick cut off. Now you have to call me a woman." The text is then superimposed on an image of Pawn Stars saying, "Best I can do is call you a dickless man."[27]

Another meme similar to this depicts a lewd cartoon where two cis-gender women are bathing in a locker room shower. One is shown fully nude from the back, the other from the front desperately trying to conceal

[24] Tijana Milosevic, *Protecting Children Online? Cyberbullying Policies of Social Media Companies* (Cambridge: MIT Press, 2018).
[25] Alessandra Grima Zoom interview by Wesley R. Bishop, May 15, 2023.
[26] Asstyn Martin Zoom interview by Wesley R. Bishop, June 24, 2021.
[27] Transphobic meme 1, first published to Instagram, accessed April 1, 2023.

their genitals and breasts, as a figure, hairy, muscular, and with an erect penis walks in and says, "Relax … I'm a woman."[28]

Instagram in both cases responded with, "We didn't remove [user's name] post."

"Because of the high volume of reports we receive, our team hasn't been able to review this post. Hate speech and symbols are not OK and are against our Community Guidelines. We're consistently working to improve our technology to remove these types of comments, including those with emojis, and disable accounts that repeatedly break our rules."[29] The text continues, recommending users simply block, mute, unfollow, or ignore harmful images. There is an option to appeal the case but doing so had no differing effect on the outcome. The hate speech remained, and Instagram's alleged Community Guidelines were permitted to be violated.

It is, of course, possible that Instagram does remove hate speech and nude images used to make such arguments, but at best it is inconsistent, and standards applied differently to different users is neither just nor conducive to creating an equitable space. Several of the participants argued that they believed the reason that fat femmes, disabled people, and people of color were targeted, while neo-Nazis and hate groups were permitted, had to do with the social identities of many of the CEOs and programmers of these companies. This reasoning makes sense, as Instagram's Community Guidelines states. Among their list of banned content, it reads:

> Instagram is a reflection of our diverse community of cultures, ages, and beliefs. We've spent a lot of time thinking about the different points of view that create a safe and open environment for everyone. We created the Community Guidelines so you can help us foster and protect this amazing community.[30]

Instagram then lists several categories such as terrorism, organized crime, illegal substances, spam, and nudity as all aspects that fall outside of approved content. Setting aside the issue of policing some of these categories more closely than others, the larger question of why terrorism and nudity are encapsulated in the same category? Instagram is very explicit in understanding that its guidelines include legitimate forms of art, body size

---

[28] Transphobic meme 2, first published to Instagram, accessed April, 1, 2023. Ibid.

[29] Instagram response as direct message to Wesley R. Bishop, April 15, 2023.

[30] Instagram Community Guidelines, Accessed April 2023. https://help.instagram.com/477434105621119.

activism, and self-expression saying, "We know that there are times when people might want to share nude images that are artistic or creative in nature, but for a variety of reasons, we don't allow nudity on Instagram. This includes photos, videos, and digitally created content that show sexual intercourse, genitals, and close-ups of fully nude buttocks."[31]

Why exactly is sex-positive, and body positive, fat-liberatory, and body-neutral nudity comparable to political movements that want to engage in genocide, suppression of civil rights, and violence? The answer is not made clear by Instagram or other sites but is perhaps a reflection of a bias in design where the latter is seen as political behavior that predominantly white men, especially those with considerable economic and political power, can engage in toward women, religious minorities, non-US citizens, and people of color. While nudity, particularly the kind that can be "artistic or creative in nature" is uncomfortable to a mainstream society that values thinness, able bodies, youth, and whiteness.

Danielle Whitfield, a body size activist and social media user who when we interviewed her identified as new to body size activism, elaborated on this more. Arguing that images and self-expression would be often heavily censored as lewd and overly sexual, men in her DMs would be permitted to continuously make comments, solicit conversations, and engage in inappropriate behavior with little recourse to stop them.

> I get offered a lot of jobs, or a lot of gigs, and stuff like that, and it's like, "Oh I need you to model lingerie." It's always something sexual. And a lot of the messages that I get and stuff like that, it's always sexual. Always sexual. You can open up my DMs later. It can be like regular pictures. I try to stay fully clothed because my account is public. I try to stay fully clothed for the most part and just show my shape, and it's still like borderline harassment. It's just disgusting … Because I'm fat, and my butt's fat, and I don't know, it's just creepy … Especially, and not even to be funny, when you're fat and you're Black you get a whole bunch of creeps, and I can't speak for anyone else, but you get a whole bunch of "Hey, ebony princess. Goddess, can I watch you eat?" kind of things, which is weird.[32]

Other participants discussed the horror of having other social media users, typically cis-men, steal their photos and use them for illegal activities. Carina Shero recounted a specific instance where one account was taking

[31] Ibid.
[32] Danielle Whitfield interview by Wesley R. Bishop, Chicago, Illinois, Nov. 4, 2019.

her photos, and then impersonating her to solicit nude photos from other users, sometimes underage girls:

> I've had people make false accounts using my likeness and material before, and Instagram really did nothing about it. One case was particularly horrible because this guy set up an account and was using it to solicit nude photos from underage girls, so he was trafficking in child pornography, and he was using my likeness to do it. It was up for five months. Instagram didn't really care, didn't do much about it. Instagram never apologized to me; they never really even emailed me about the situation. They just finally gave me access to the account, and I had to spend all this time writing to people explaining the situation, shutting down the site, etc.[33]

Vivienne Rose, a Texas-based model, adult entertainer, and body size activist recounted how such loss of identity can be the direct result of harassment and retaliation (Fig. 2.1). "One of [my accounts was] hacked … because I didn't give him [the man messaging her] attention."[34] Rose was required to create another account, rely on friends, and make repeated appeals to Instagram who finally simply deleted the account. All of her work, her space on the platform, and very identity was hijacked as a result of harassment, and the only recourse was simply to erase her presence, her work, and leave her the option to start again. "It hurts because you put so much work [into those accounts] … it takes time to build. You put a lot of yourself into those accounts. So, you just … You lose all hope for five seconds. And then you create a new one. You're like, 'Damn it.'"[35]

Shero's experience of encountering graphic and disturbing content in her direct messages highlights the distressing reality faced by many individuals, including our participants, on social media platforms. The prevalence of images depicting violence, cruelty, and explicit content not only creates a hostile environment but also poses serious psychological and emotional risks to users. This issue goes beyond mere inconvenience or discomfort—it directly affects the mental well-being and safety of

[33] Wesley Bishop and Carina Shero "Instagram Deleted Her Account @ Over 400K Followers: Fat Phobia in Art and Social Media, and How Carina Shero Continues to Fight for Better Representation of All Bodies," *TERSE*, April 15, 2018, https://tersejournal.com/2018/04/19/instagram-deleted-her-account-over-400k-followers-fat-phobia-in-art-and-social-media-and-how-carina-shero-continues-to-fight-for-better-representation-of-all-bodies/.

[34] Vivienne Rose interview by Wesley R. Bishop, Indianapolis, Indiana, May 20, 2021.

[35] Ibid.

Fig. 2.1 Model and activist Vivienne Rose poses for a picture. She explained that the act of taking and posting pictures of her body online helped her develop a healthier and more loving relationship with her self-image

individuals such as Shero who rely on these platforms for professional connections and opportunities. The failure of social media companies, including Instagram, to effectively address and mitigate such disturbing messages is a stark reminder of their negligence and disregard for user protection.

Research on the impact of online harassment and exposure to violent imagery further emphasizes the gravity of this issue. Studies have shown that repeated exposure to graphic content can lead to increased levels of anxiety, depression, and post-traumatic stress symptoms. The psychological toll inflicted upon individuals who are subjected to such distressing material cannot be understated.[36]

Addressing this problem requires a multifaceted approach involving stricter content moderation, improved reporting mechanisms, and increased accountability from social media platforms. It is imperative that platforms like Instagram take proactive measures to combat the circulation of harmful and explicit content, ensuring the safety and well-being of their users. Only through robust enforcement of community guidelines, effective algorithms, and responsive support systems can we begin to alleviate the distress caused by online harassment and the exposure to disturbing imagery.

The pervasive culture of online harassment and derogatory comments, as exemplified by the quote, "Nobody wants to be unhealthy. It's your laziness that [is] holding you back from a healthy life and these types of stuff are making those who are very lazy to put some effort on themselves to become comfortable in their laziness and hide the fault they are doing"[37] demonstrates a disturbing trend within the online work environment. These comments, coupled with the illegal harassment have become part of an online work environment that does little to protect activists, marginalized workers, and users, but that protects puritanical sensibilities, white male aggression, and profits. In later chapters we will explore specifically how online platforms have developed technologies to automatically censure these fat women for their work, their activism, and their persistent demand that they be recognized and include these individuals in our cultural representations and discourse.

---

[36] Anthony Feinstein, Blair Audet, and Elizabeth Waknine, "Witnessing Images of Extreme Violence: A Psychological Study of Journalists in the Newsroom," *JRSM Open* 5 (no. 8, 2014), 1–7. Carolyn Gregoire, "What Constant Exposure to Negative News is Doing to Our Mental Health," *HuffPost*, Feb. 19, 2015. Accessed December 21, 2023. https://www.huffpost.com/entry/violent-media-anxiety_n_6671732. Shana Gadarian, "How Sensationalist TV Stories on Terrorism Make Americans More Hawkish," *Washington Post*, Oct. 9, 2014. Accessed December 21, 2023. https://www.washingtonpost.com/news/monkey-cage/wp/2014/10/09/how-sensationalist-tv-stories-on-terrorism-make-americans-more-hawkish/.

[37] Comment left on Instagram, screenshot Wesley R. Bishop, Jan. 18, 2023.

CHAPTER 3

Media and the Ideal Body

Abstract This chapter looks at the differences and similarities between social media and traditional forms of media as it relates to body diversity representation. Participants argued that the similarity in traditional media and social media was in the numerous instances of anti-fat bias in characters, stories, advertisements, and basic assumptions. Participants also discussed the issue of the body positivity movement being co-opted by both corporations and thin-to-average-size white women. Conversation often turned to well-known figures such as Ashley Graham, Lizzo, Tess Holiday, and popular narratives about fatness in clothing, marketing, etc. Participants discussed the limits to body positivity, while also disagreeing with the ability to use a body neutrality movement for positive change. Instead, the majority of the participants stated that fat liberation was needed, and that where body positivity or body neutrality could be used was in very-limited-to-no circumstances.

Keywords Co-optation • Body positivity • Fat liberation • Celebrity • Corporate capitalism • Media • BBW • SSBBW • Sex work • Porn • OnlyFans

Carina Shero, activist, artist, and co-founder of the Femme FATales. Her work focuses on showing fat bodies in sensual and sexy framing to challenge anti-fat bias in art and aesthetics.

INTRODUCTION

The co-optation of fat liberation into the body positive movement has been a topic of much discussion in recent years. For example, Aubrey Gordon argues:

> Though countless new supporters have flocked to the body positivity movement in the last two decades, few are aware of its considerably more radical roots in fat activism, and fewer still seem to have any commitment to justice

work that extends beyond their personal relationship to their own body. Even body positivity's newer substitute, body neutrality, is designed to right individuals' relationships with their own bodies, but not to change the cultural context that has created such widespread discrimination against fat people, and such negative body image in people of all sizes.[1]

Other critics have charged that aside from focusing on "feel-good" emotions, the body positive movement is also dangerously focused on the feeling of thin to mid-size white women, completely ignoring the issues of women of color, people with disabilities, and fat people who are prevented from taking up space in public, being hired for jobs, and moving about the world unaccosted.[2]

However, not everyone agrees that the body positive movement is a total failure. Despite the criticisms, writers such as Lindy West and Sonya Renee Taylor have argued that self-love, focus on personal psychological states, and affirmation is important to any liberation for fat people.[3]

During the interviews we found that participants mirrored this diverse set of opinions about body positivity, body neutrality, and fat liberation. We concluded that although there were certain common concerns or focal points, no two individuals completely mirrored one another in either the way they viewed the different aspects of these movements or the best ways to address those concerns. As such we opted to use "body size activism" to describe the various aspects of participants' thinking. We define body size activism as a conceived field of resistance to body shame, marginalization, and pathologizing and punishing fat people. In this sense, body size activism relates to other body-based forms of social activism, such as the broader field of disability rights activism, and challenges both internal and

---

[1] Aubrey Gordon, "How 'Body Positivity' Got Hijacked by Brands and Influencers," *Self,* Jan. 9, 2023. Accessed December 21, 2023. https://www.self.com/story/aubrey-gordon-book-excerpt.
[2] Viren Swami, "Why the Body Positivity Movement Risks Turning Toxic," *The Conversation*, Sept. 14, 2022. Accessed, December 21, 2023. https://theconversation.com/why-the-body-positivity-movement-risks-turning-toxic-189913.
[3] Lindy West, *Shrill: Notes from a Loud Woman* (New York: Hachette Books, 2016). Sonya Renee Taylor, *The Body Is Not an Apology: The Power of Radical Self-Love* (Los Angeles: Berrett-Koehler Publishers, 2018).

external policing of bodies on the basis of size, appearance, health, and aesthetics.

In this chapter we break down these conversations to examine how participants thought about the co-optation of fat liberation's message in the body positive movement, how body positivity in turn has been co-opted by celebrities and corporations, how this fits into the broader issue of media's troubling treatment of fat bodies historically, and finally why participants were skeptical about the usefulness of body neutrality as an end goal or simultaneous movement with fat liberation.

Interestingly, despite the varying sentiments expressed by participants toward these figures, corporate campaigns, and the notion of body positivity as a derivative of fat liberation in body size activism, a consensus emerged. Participants agreed that the issues represented by these figures and campaigns were interconnected with anti-fat bias and the diversion of attention from the fundamental needs of fat individuals, such as access to clothing, medical care, transportation, and, finally, positive media representations.

CO-OPTATION: CELEBRITY, CORPORATE CAPITALISM, AND MEDIA

Participants generally believed that newer forms of social media, particularly on different platforms that were image based, permitted a far more diverse creation of images of different body types. That is, social media platforms due to their user content creation models naturally led to new representations in art, specifically in portraying human bodies. Yet this increase in body diversity collided with the issue of co-optation, particularly in the context of fat liberation, being assimilated into the more marketable and capitalist-friendly "body positive movement."

We asked the participants to identify the key figures in this co-optation and discuss the specific concerns associated with it. The three principal figures during this time were the models Ashley Graham, Tess Holiday, and the musical artist Lizzo. This exploration led to a broader discussion of how the principles of fat liberation and anti-racism temper and differentiate the criticism of these figures as fat people. Participants acknowledged the necessity of recognizing that tearing down certain figures, even when they exhibit problematic aspects, can ultimately harm the overarching cause and foster a toxic culture of unattainable perfection. Furthermore, we explored the criticisms directed toward these individuals and trends, questioning whether they were intended to spur boycotts or to initiate "cancel culture." The responses varied greatly, and participants hesitated to propose a universal solution to this complex issue.

As Jessie Oliver said, "Ashley Graham has said outrightly fat shaming stuff. I mean she said things like, "Well I'm plus sized but not unhealthy." Right, there's that health word again. She also, I mean Ashley Graham kind of does some trash things in general. It's hard to separate. For me it's hard to separate out the things she does as a human versus … her as a plus size model. I think again, we get back to this idea of that plus representation is someone who is a size twelve. Like is that actual representation? And quite frankly is that actually really plus sized, right? She is still significantly smaller than the average-size woman in this country."[4]

Robina Strowder echoed this concern about Graham, saying:

> I think [many] have appropriated the body positive movement. I think that is absolutely true. I think that they now want to capitalize off of the plus-size dollar because they know that we will buy it, and we will make that shit look good. They know that we want it now, and so I feel like … For example, let's go with the Vicky Secret. I know they just released their size fourteen model after the fact of [their] president …[saying]… "Victoria's Secret will never use a plus-size model," or will never have a plus-size angel … This happened after … this man said out of his mouth, "We will never," and because the fat people who had never been able to shop in there before stopped buying their perfume … and the soaps and the stuff that smells good, took so much sales away from them … So now they want to come back with a size fourteen model…. I mean, no shade no tea, but there is a lot of plus-size models who don't even want the term plus … in front of their name … You know [who] I'm going to say … Ashley Graham. I don't fuck with her. I'm sorry. I don't rock with it … She doesn't want to be associated with the plus-size industry … We made her. We made her. She walked for Lane Bryant and had her booty shaking on the runway, and we took that wench to the top because we were sharing, we were reposting, we were saying, "Yes, this is what we want to see," … and what's she do? As soon as she got a contract for real for real, she lost what, forty pounds? Then she's like, "I'm not plus-size anymore. I'm just a model." I think people claim it when it's convenient because they know that they need our support.

---

[4] Jessie Oliver interview by Wesley R. Bishop, Chicago, Illinois, Nov. 4, 2019.

As Strowder explained, this anger with figures such as Graham was more than just someone claiming something they were not; instead, it misled and made a mockery of a real issue that fat people had been fighting against for quite some time—namely, access to basic commercial goods like clothing:

> For instance, when Ashley Graham came out with her swimsuit line or when her collab with *Swimsuits For All*, then it was, "This is for everybody. This is plus size," but I mean to be honest it's not. It runs ridiculously small. So, it's not, but that's what she will market towards to feel like she's supportive of us as much as we were supportive of her … I think that they are just giving us a piece of the cookie. They want us to be quiet. Because they see the ruckus that we're causing. They see that we demand more options, and so they say, "Here's a little bit. We'll give you to a size twenty or a size twenty-two, but if you all don't buy it, then we ain't doing nothing else after that" … You know, they will say brands who have had plus-size, and they will say, "Oh yeah, we got plus-size, but it's online only." So fat people don't go to the store? That's a major issue for me. That is a huge issue for me. I hate shopping online because I have a bigger body; I have to try my clothes on. I have to know how they fit me, or else I don't want to buy. The fact that I can't just wake up and say, "Dang, I want a new outfit tonight," for it to be of any type of style or fashion of anything, I can't just go into the store and get it. It's crazy to me.[5]

Saucye West, too, expressed similar concerns:

> Yeah, absolutely … people like Ashley Graham, Rosy Mercado. I think that they definitely have benefited from this community. There's an old saying, "Don't bite the hand that feeds you." These people definitely used [the fat] community when they were coming up. They used the platform of body positivity and got big and left communities. And a lot of people who may not even know the internalized fatphobia that they're dealing with, that may not even know their own internal struggles when it comes to their body, they don't know that that's trauma. [So] when someone who they adored and they love leaves the behind but they're still holding on to them. They're still like, "I'm still going to buy everything that she does, but …" but when she left you behind, she literally said, "I don't want to be this no more." I don't want to be associated with this ….

[5] Robina Strowder interview by Wesley R. Bishop, Chicago, Illinois, Nov. 4, 2019.

The matter of representation, then, and claiming aspects of oneself, such as fatness, is essential in this line of thinking. To use aspects such as body size, implicitly and explicitly for one's brand or in media in general comes with a basic ethical principle that one will at least do no harm to that community and at best advocate for social concerns in that group.

Noting the issues between body positivity generally and fat liberation specifically Carina Shero elaborated this point. If body positivity, as a specific part of body size activism, was to have any value, then it was going to require a radical shift in thinking about how we as a society view and accept bodies:

> For instance, take Ashley Graham. You'll see multiple magazines saying "Ashley Graham is a Body Positive Icon" when she really is not a beacon for the body positive community. She gave an interview once where she said, "Oh, there are some mornings when I feel fat." Well, news flash, we actually are fat. Every single day. This is nothing we can escape. This is just who we are. So the way people like Graham and others frame bodies is through a negative frame. And she has gained her notoriety off of the backs of actual fat people who for years and years have been putting themselves out there for body positivity and a huge part of her fan base are people who are actually fat. Her being a person who is an "inbetweenie" size, who therefore has a privilege of being on all these magazine covers because she is "acceptable," and then shitting all over her fan base is the antithesis of what the body positive movement should be about. For example, Graham is currently on a TV show called *Revenge Body* which is a program that in essence tells you there is something inherently wrong with certain types of bodies that you then have to move away from to get a "better body." There is nothing wrong with anyone's body. Ever. You know? … So that goes against the entire idea of body positivity. And so, I could name many other people who have done similar things where they have said "Oh, body positive!" but in actuality, no. If we really want to dissect this false presentation, it is not only NOT body positivity, but is harming the whole message of body positivity.[6]

---

[6]Wesley Bishop and Carina Shero "Instagram Deleted Her Account @ Over 400K Followers: Fat Phobia in Art and Social Media, and How Carina Shero Continues to Fight for Better Representation of All Bodies," *TERSE*, April 15, 2018. https://tersejournal.com/2018/04/19/instagram-deleted-her-account-over-400k-followers-fat-phobia-in-art-and-social-media-and-how-carina-shero-continues-to-fight-for-better-representation-of-all-bodies/.

Saucye West included Lizzo in this criticism, saying, "She definitely came out the box saying certain things and being a certain way to fatness. But then when she is going into the next level in her life," West argued she felt as if Lizzo had tried to distance herself from the movement, and to an extent the fat community by claiming that she was not an activist because of her body size or race. "You can do whatever you want to do with your body," West argued, "but just because you go into a different lane with how you feel about your body and what you want to do with your body and then you say from ... David Letterman that 'I didn't sign up to be a fat activist, I didn't sign up to be a fat liberationist.' And what were you doing? What exactly were you doing then?"[7]

It is of note, though, that when discussing certain figures such as Lizzo and Tess Holiday there was a more cautious criticism. Part of this was reflected in the participants not wanting to put down large fat individuals, who they thought represented real progress in body size acceptance, but also because in some of the participants' thinking there had to be some room to allow grace for people who did not know what they were doing. For them this did not excuse past actions that harmed the fat community, or set back body size activism, but it at least provided a way to not be too severe from a celebrity who was actively learning and helping the fat community.

As Jessie Oliver said:

> Then we get Tess Holliday who I really struggle with Tess Holliday because there's a part of me that was like, this is the first time someone in a truly fat body has actually crossed that threshold. And I think that's important. And I think that visibility is important and I appreciate that, but also there's been some bad business practices of taking money and not providing things based on the money they took and just saying some things that are just like questionably ignorant things to say. But I do think, I guess also it's hard. Those are both people who went into being a model and then to hold them to an accountability of social activism. Is that a weird 2019 construct that we're in that sometimes people didn't realize that that was also what they were signing up for? Do you know what I mean? Is that an unrealistic, unfair expectation on the consumer end, right? I don't know. I don't know. I really don't know how to answer that. But I do know that I struggle with both of those individuals. Some of the things they have said and done, Ashley Graham I just think is, I mean she touches people without consent. She does things is

---

[7] Saucye West Zoom interview by Wesley R. Bishop, Aug. 5, 2021.

like appropriative and weird in general and I have a problem with that. And Tess Holliday, I just think everything about certain situations she got in over her head and I just don't think she understood what she was doing. Not that that excuses things. But like, I don't know, in a world where we can try and figure out … I don't know.[8]

Other participants agreed, particularly with Tess Holiday who they saw as a major breakthrough in modeling. But they added that it could not be ignored that figures like Tess Holiday, although fat, were beautiful, white, and as a result had privileges and limits to whom they could accurately be said to be representing. This was not just an issue with one model, but an entire industry that worked within conceptions of desire, and even when marginalized bodies were represented they were still portrayed as unattainable.

Barthelemy expounded on this point, thinking through how particularly as a Latina woman "body diversity" was really a particular shape, commonly known as "hourglass," that was hypersexualized and still unattainable:

Right now, in the media, when you think body positivity, it's a skinny girl hunching over and like, "Oh I have rolls. Look at me, so normal." So you see a lot of that and it's disheartening because it's all like, there's this whole other, other group of people who like, I don't have to crouch over, I have roles just naturally. And I feel also with media, they have this preconceived notion of what beauty should be. And it's like, oh, if you're going to be plus size, you have to have the hour[glass] shape figure … yeah, you have to have a flat tummy and an ass and perky boobs. And it's rare that anyone can get to that or whatever. And I think having that kind of image portrayed in the media, it's not attainable … I think it's great that women like Tess Holiday and Ashley Graham are making breakthroughs and able to do things that other models weren't able to do. I think it's great that these women are doing these things, but I also would like to see women of color as well. Again, my biggest thing, and I don't follow them on Instagram anymore, specifically for that reason. It feels like when they do it, it's unattainable because it's all like, you don't look like me. You're not quite shaped like me. I'm never going to look like Ashley Graham. I'm never going to look like Tess Holiday. It's unattainable for me. So I don't follow them. I think it's great what they're doing and they're out there and they're able to be a small representation of the plus size community. But again, you don't really rep-

---

[8] Oliver interview, Nov. 4, 2019.

resent me. When I see Latina models, again, it's the hourglass, the ones that look like Ashley Graham basically. And it's like, but you don't look like me. I would love to see more women of color and more women of body shapes in these modeling campaigns or breaking through and things like that. The biggest one right now is Lizzo. I love Lizzo and it's nice to see a woman of color, not quite an hourglass shape, doing it and doing it on her own terms. Yeah.[9]

Asstyn Marin worried, however, that in the move to criticize these figures that the body size activist movement would not become too exclusive. She said she followed the celebrities discussed here, including Ashley Graham. Her concerns were both that consumers of media were expecting fully thought activism from celebrities and, more importantly, that thin body ideals were a policing mechanism that impacted all women psychologically:

I was raised in a time where being curvy was not popular, [it] was not a good thing, So it depends on the environment you were raised in as well. I don't think that there's anything wrong with a woman who's a size twelve, embracing the body positivity movement, because her whole life, she may have been told she was fat. Because [she may have] used to be much smaller. And I remember people making negative comments about my body when I was, 150-160 pounds. I was younger. So I feel like there's ... I mean body positivity should really be for everybody. I see a lot of quibbles on TikToK especially, with mid size women and plus size women and all of that. And I don't really think that it's a good thing to be too critical of those mid-sized ladies. Because like I said, there are a lot of us who were raised by women with disordered eating and their own body issues. I had a mother, I love my mother and she never really gave me a hard time about my weight or anything, but I saw her barely eating. I saw her, putting moral value on food and things like that. So you don't know the environment some of these people were brought up in.[10]

In late 2022, however, fashion reporters began noting that perhaps the heyday of body diversity may already be on the wane before it even began. Periodizing the phenomena of more mainstream body acceptance as taking off in the 2010s and continuing through into the 2020s, fashion writers discussed how many high-end brands were attempting to pivot away

[9] Jackie Barthelemy interview by Wesley R. Bishop, Chicago, Illinois, Nov. 1, 2019.
[10] Asstyn Martin Zoom interview by Wesley R. Bishop, June 24, 2021.

from newly made commitments to be more size inclusive in both representation of body types in models and making clothing for a wider array of body sizes. As Tariro Mzezewa reported in *The Cut* in March 2023:

> Even though over the past decade there has been an increase in the visibility of plus-size models like Ashley Graham, Paloma Elsesser, Alva Claire, and others alongside the thin models on runways, suggesting that the industry was becoming more inclusive, it turns out that the fashion industry still needs to do a much better job regarding size inclusivity on the runway. This past fashion season, there was chatter about the return of ultrathin models to the runway. Watching show after show, it seemed that the fashion industry was doing worse in terms of body-size representation. If you found yourself wondering if there were fewer plus-size models on the runways, you weren't wrong. Data collected by *Vogue Business* and published this week proves that to be true.[11]

In response to this, fat activists, body positive social media accounts, and concerned members of the fashion industry began sharing posts with the #MyBodyIsNotATrend and other testimonies, links, and stories about how the fashion industry could not erase the modest gains made in the past ten years.

Saucye West discussed this back-and-forth between progress and regression in body size acceptance for fat bodies and argued that this precariousness made celebrity figures potential activists to advance a cause or opponents to fat liberation. To her there was no real neutral ground, and criticism needed to be voiced to establish a base line of what was and was not acceptable for people to do when speaking about fat bodies:

> I think the main thing was when [Ashley Graham] said, "I just don't want to be known as a plus size model anymore." It changed and it shift the paradigm within fashion and plus-size because you have all these other brands talking about, "Well, maybe we should just drop the plus because this was going on and this person doesn't want to be affiliated and maybe we could just try to be in, mesh in with straight body." No, we can't do that. However, you want to. It sounds amazing. But straight size people don't deal with the same stuff. They do not deal with the same things. But when you just say, "You know what? I'm just going to go, I'm going to drop it. And I'm just

[11] Tariro Mzezewa, "What Happened to the Plus-Size Models?" *The Cut*, March 14, 2023. Accessed June 1, 2023. https://www.thecut.com/2023/03/what-happened-to-the-plus--size-models.html

going to be, I just want to be a model." And so when you drop that, you don't just drop it in word, you drop it in mind. So that means whatever you do in your career, you don't care about anybody that you left behind. So that includes her doing any kind of collaboration. She's not going to fight to have any explicit sizes in her collaborations. She's not going to fight to have visibly fat models and things. She's not going to fight. She's not. And she's probably going to critique us even harder. She's like, "Well, I'm in this, I'm on this stage blah, blah." No. And I think that her doing that, it just set off this jacked up domino effect within the industry. It took us several steps back from where we were.[12]

OLDER FORMS OF MEDIA AND BODY SHAME

Older forms of media, such as print and television, have long been noted by fat studies researchers for their overwhelming anti-fat bias. Scholars have extensively discussed and analyzed the abundance of stories, characters, and visual media that perpetuate this bias. The pervasive nature of this bias underscores the need for critical examination and transformation within these media platforms.

The use of popular fat cartoon characters such as Homer Simpson and Ursula the Sea Witch as caricatures illustrates this bias. These characters are often portrayed as lazy, unintelligent, or evil and greedy. Such depictions reinforce a sense of morality in which fat bodies are used to argue that individuals belonging to a particular community have deviated from virtuous standards. The documentation of this popular moral framework and the association of fatness with moral decline have been extensively studied.[13]

Participants in the interviews expressed the desire for inclusive and authentic representation in media. They emphasized the importance of media that does not portray fat individuals as constantly striving to be something other than their current selves or as inherently sad. One participant, Jessie Oliver, drew attention to the portrayal of Sadness as a fat blob in the Disney Pixar film *Inside Out*, suggesting that this perpetuates the limited representation of fat bodies and contributes to negative stereotypes that fat people are miserable, not joyous, and that fat equals

---

[12] West interview, Aug. 5, 2021.
[13] Kathleen LeBesco, *Revolting Bodies?: The Struggle to Redefine Fat Identity* (Amherst: University of Massachusetts Press, 2003); Aubrey Gordon, *What We Don't Talk About When We Talk About Fat* (Boston: Beacon Press, 2020); West, *Shrill*.

depression and misery. Likewise, television shows such as *This Is Us* and *Mike and Molly*, which center on characters attending Overeaters Anonymous, reinforce the idea that fat people can only find companionship and happiness within their own community, and that loving a fat person is a form of "settling" since no thin to mid-range-sized person could ever love a fat person. "There should be a space for us," Oliver stated:

> We deserve representation in media. We deserve representation in media that isn't portraying us as desperate to be something other than what we currently are. Or sad. I mean I talk about this because it bothers me so much. I've talked about some podcasts. What is that movie? What is it called? *Inside Out* … The portrayal of sadness is literally a fat blob. We train people to see fat bodies that way when we do not offer them any other option or you look at something like *This Is Us*, which I refuse to watch. And *Mike and Molly*, which have the same construct of two fat people meeting at Overeaters Anonymous. That somehow our lives must be dismissed into, fat people only belong with other fat people. Fat people are always trying to be something other than fat. And fat people are sad about their lives. There's very few representations of joy and fat joy. And that is a problem … This idea that fat people aren't having sex is bonkers because if 67% of the women in this country are fat, we're having sex. Because it's just like mathematically we're all having sex. Right? Yeah. So it's just like, when we are combating a larger media, self-produced media becomes imperative. Right.[14] These narratives suggest that fat individuals are always trying to transform themselves and are inherently dissatisfied with their lives. The lack of joyful representations of fat bodies in media poses a significant problem that needs to be addressed.

For the participants, and many other fat activists in their writing and studies, it is crucial to challenge and dismantle the prevailing notion that fat individuals are excluded from positive experiences such as relationships and intimacy. Participants aptly pointed out the fallacy of assuming that fat people are not engaging in sexual relationships by referencing their own past experiences. With a significant percentage of the population being fat, the idea that fat individuals are not sexually active is not only baseless and cruel, but also a patently false claim. It is prejudice persisting in the face of empirical data. The absence of diverse representations perpetuates these harmful stereotypes and reinforces societal biases. In the face of such a

[14] Oliver interview, Nov. 4, 2019.

media landscape, self-produced media becomes imperative in reclaiming narratives and showcasing diverse experiences. Carina Shero argued this in discussing films such as *Shallow Hal* and the notorious *What's Eating Gilbert Grape*:

> Think about it. How many movies do you know where there is a main character that is my size and the movie is not about their weight? Not one of those films that a skinny girl wakes up in a fat girl's body, and the movie is about her freaking out. Or that is not about the person being comedic relief. There is no movie where there is someone my size and it is not specifically about their size. It's just not a thing. I remember watching *Empire* for the first time and seeing Gabourey Sidibe in a bomb ass outfit looking so fine, and seeing how they had given her the best wardrobe, and seeing that they would represent this fat woman of color in the best way possible ... the first time I ever saw something like that on TV I was just like, "Hell. Fucking. Yes." And that is why I have to keep doing this because I want to try and give others the same experience. I see how in any comment section there are people just ripping Sidibe apart ... just for existing. We have to keep going so there isn't just one person.[15]

MEDIA FORMS AND FIGURES THAT CHALLENGE

Identifying the problem, however, is only a beginning to address the issue. The next step will need to be representing diverse body types, such as fat bodies, in a positive light. In this fashion, body size activism intersects with other body-based forms of activism such as demands within the disability rights movement, sex positivity, and the destigmatization of mental health. Here, many of the participants who worked as models saw their work as most effective in terms of activism. By creating images, modeling, and working in the fashion industry they argued they were creating that much-needed positive image of fat bodies. Social media, therefore, was a significant component in this activism as it allows fat models to create images, free themselves of unwanted anti-fat narratives, and show how fat people are beautiful, whole, complete people. Saucye West discussed this,

---

[15] Wesley Bishop and Carina Shero "Instagram Deleted Her Account @ Over 400K Followers: Fat Phobia in Art and Social Media, and How Carina Shero Continues to Fight for Better Representation of All Bodies," *TERSE*, April 15, 2018. https://tersejournal.com/2018/04/19/instagram-deleted-her-account-over-400k-followers-fat-phobia-in-art-and-social-media-and-how-carina-shero-continues-to-fight-for-better-representation-of-all-bodies/.

arguing she understood early on the power that could come from being a fat, Black woman model:

> I wanted to be a model since I was a young girl, but I didn't think that was possible, the older I got and the fatter I got, I didn't see anyone who looked like me as a model. But with the emergence of plus-sized modeling, and I began to see people … they still didn't look like me, but they were still bigger than what I had ever seen. And when I think of people, I was like, "Well this … It's a possibility for me. There's another … There is a world out there that I can make my own lane." And when I decided to do that, I had to … because when you're on Instagram and you're just being a regular girl, you're just posting you and your friend, I have a daughter, I'm with my family … but I had to do a rebranding of myself and say, "I'm going to be very fashion and fashion centric and fat activist centric." And what I'm doing and being really bold in how I'm putting it out there … so instead of me just taking a selfie in a swimsuit, I felt like it was more liberating to me to show my entire body as opposed to full body pic of me in a swimsuit, just to show an inspiration as well as being political about what I can do in this body and what is possible for everyone to do in this body.[16]

The emergence of plus-sized modeling opened doors for those who previously felt marginalized and invisible in the fashion industry. Representation sparked a sense of possibility and empowerment. The rebranding process and the intentional focus on fashion and fat activism reflect a bold and deliberate effort to carve out a space for diverse bodies in the media landscape. Vivienne Rose argued the same, claiming, "I think social media is still saturated with body ideal. What the media shows, it's still all over the place. It's still in flash photography. It's something that we're bombarded with, so having those other images out there, it creates a counterpoint. It shows an alternate reality that after enough times being posted [also becomes] a reality. So, you have those girls that are out there with you perceivably unattainable ideals, the filters and all of that. But then you have the girls posting real you and make-up free, the men and women and whatever gender they identify as out there breaking those norms and showing that this is their norm and it doesn't matter what media says it should be."[17]

---

[16]West interview, Aug. 5, 2021.
[17]Vivienne Rose interview by Wesley R. Bishop, Indianapolis, Indiana, May 20, 2021.

Deborah L. Tolman, a psychologist specializing in adolescent development, emphasizes the impact of media on young people, stating, "Media messages regarding body image can significantly influence adolescents' self-perception, leading to body dissatisfaction and increased risk of disordered eating behaviors."[18] These insights highlight the significance of figures who challenge traditional beauty norms and the need for diverse representation in the media landscape. Saucye West continued:

> There was a model in particular. Her name was Mia Amber ... I remember she was in this movie, [*Road Trip*,] it was about college guys or whatever. And she ended up being with ... a really small, really white guy ... [laughs]... Yes. So she was the first one I had seen that looked ... as far as being in a darker hue and being super curvy. And so when I saw her ... I was like, "Oh my God, I can possibly get into this world. I could possibly lay [claim and] wiggle myself in here." I don't want to mention this other person, but I will mention her, but I see Ashley Graham, as well, coming up. And I also see models like Tess Holiday ... and Tess was the one who was the biggest person to come into this industry and make a wave. If Amber was still alive, I think that she would have absolutely done so much. But Tess was the one to do it and, of course, you know how that goes, but she did pave the way and let people see that fat bodies can be in fashion ... And so I was like, Well, I want to be the Black version of that, basically. I want to be the Black version of a super top model.' And that was pretty much what my goal was. Seeing white faces in this industry getting all of the glory and I'm just like, "I don't see anybody that's Black doing this."[19]

Mia Amber's presence as a darker-skinned, curvy model made a lasting impression, inspiring the participant to envision her own possibilities within the industry.

Laura Weetzie Wilson, a participant in the study, shared her personal experiences that shaped her understanding of body image and fat acceptance. Her experiences with body image stigmas in the world of modern dance and her involvement in the 4th Trimester Bodies Project. The 4th Trimester project, specifically, worked to photograph recent mothers with their babies and explore how they felt about parenthood and their bodies after giving birth. Wilson explained that with both the issues of

---

[18] Deborah L. Tolman, *Dilemmas of Desire: Teenage Girls Talk about Sexuality* (Cambridge: Harvard University Press, 2002).
[19] West interview, Aug. 5, 2021.

hypersexualizing nudity and anti-fat bias, the project, which was meant to be a way for people to explore feelings of their bodies and move toward acceptance, often became an argument over censorship, particularly in online platforms such as Instagram and other photo-sharing sites:

> I was really involved in modern dance in West Virginia and had a modern dance … troupe. And … that's where I learned about a lot of body image stuff, and a lot of the stigmas with body image. Because we went to the dance adjudication and for the West Virginia Dance Festival, one of the judges said to one of our dancers, "Don't put her up in the air, she's too big for that." Even though like the whole piece was around her being put up in the air, and it was totally fine. They said no one wants to see a big body up in the air. And I was just like … that … stuck with me as far as like how much pushback there is and how much you've got to fight to creatively be seen.
>
> And then years later after college and everything, I moved to Chicago and I wasn't really involved in much until … around 2012 it was when my friends started the *4th Trimester Bodies Project*, and it was really about mostly mothers and parents and how they relate to their bodies postpartum. And that's where I kind of learned about the body positive movement in the beginnings of it for me was through that. And just seeing the reaction of people's ability to see themselves clearly and like what do bigger bodies look like even …. objectively because we were publishing, or we were putting [the photos] online through on Instagram and on our webpage bodies up through like about a size eighteen at the time … [and] all these people were saying, "Well why aren't you showing any bigger bodies?"
>
> … And then when we finally in the first couple months of the project, got someone in that had a larger body, like I don't know, I want to say like a size twenty-four or something that everyone was like, "Oh this project is for everybody." And then even that person who [we] finally photographed that was larger, she was like, "Well, if I'm not the kind of body you're looking for that I don't have to even come into the studio, just tell me that you don't want me." And we were like, "No, get in here you're exactly what we need. This is what we need." We need to see of all shapes and sizes so that we can feel comfortable ….
>
> So, it was through that movement through working on that project … that I became really active in the movement and much more loud and we had a lot of discrimination, like censorship … because not only were we putting bodies in bras and underwear, we were showing, even though no genitals were almost ever shown, the kids [who] were always naked. It was black and white photographs. And so, people had either … a problem with the kids being naked online even though … they were being held by their

parents and there was nothing shown, or they had a problem with especially larger bodies being shown without airbrushing.[20]

Wilson went on to explain that for her she then spent the next years after that deepening her understanding and art, as both a dancer and a visual artist, to understand not just a shallow body positivity but a more radical fat liberation outlook:

> Yeah, so at first it was a very rudimentary idea that's just like all bodies are good and one of our things is all bodies are beautiful and was very just kind of like everyone has a place and everyone is okay here and blah blah blah. But as time went on … I was … realiz[ing] how marginalized certain aspects of society are … you need to make room for [fat people], and the less they're represented, the less radical or interesting or helpful the movement is. So, it really became over the course of like five or six years, very much more fat positivity than just like generic body positivity because it's really about moving over and making room for fat bodies. Like I mean I don't want to sound harsh, but like we don't need more, "everyone deserves to feel comfortable in their body" … we don't need more acceptance of a size to like they're already accepted, they just need to move over. So, it became more of a fat positivity and learning all the different ways that there's discrimination of fat bodies and how rampant and deep in society it is to be discriminated against because of your size. So that's how it's changed for me. It's become a lot more radical and a lot more … It's a lot more important to really see and embrace the largest of all the bodies. That is where we need and that's where the work needs to be done.[21]

From a more general body acceptance, then, to a more radical fat liberation model, many of the participants described a similar process of moving from psychologically accepting their own bodies, and celebrating them, to a more radical and political stance of demanding accessibility for fat people. Anti-fat bias was seen as the main issue with this lack of civil liberties and access to clothing, and media representation. This anti-fat bias, though, was understood as an intersectional phenomenon that was rooted in white supremacy, capitalistic exploitation, and anti-sex/pleasure impulses.

---

[20] Laura Weetzie Wilson interview by Wesley R. Bishop, Chicago, Illinois, Nov. 4, 2019.
[21] Ibid.

Vivienne Rose discussed this, arguing that even within the fat community an anti-porn and anti-sex-worker attitude hampered body-based activism and worker's rights in general. Specifically, Rose described her issues with some in the fat community shunning the BBW (big beautiful women) marker because it was associated with porn. "We're being challenged to create more categories," Rose stated as she explained how the rise of some models like Tess Holiday and Ashley Graham made people realize that there were different experiences for people of different sizes even if they were all placed under the umbrella term "fat." "Plus size is just a heading," she said. "There are many subtitles beneath. There's SSBBW [super-size big, beautiful women]. There's BBW. There's just plain fat."[22] Although she could understand the issues around fetishization she simply did not see the problem with a term being associated with the porn industry and why that would make it a negative. "Now that I'm in my wrapped old age of forty-three, I am not afraid of sexuality … I think that some other narratives need to be challenged first to let us [accept] BBW and not categorically make [the claim] "oh, I'm not associated with porn." Because you know what, we all have sex. We all masturbate. [BBW does get] used in porn and yes, I have heard that plenty that they hate BBW because it's associated with porn, but it's again just a descriptor if you don't give it any power."[23]

Vivienne Rose's line of argument fits into the broader context of concerns around what Women's Studies scholar Meredith Ralston has called "whorephobia." "We need to destigmatize sex," she writes. "Especially for women."[24] Ralston is critical of feminists, especially women, who police women's sexuality and especially their ability to use their body as they see fit, including working in the adult entertainment industry. Ralston discusses Victoria Bateman, a professor at Cambridge University who has gained notoriety for her embrace of nudism. Bateman has argued that one is truly comfortable with their body if they are able to play recreational sports completely in the buff. "[Bateman] could play volleyball in the nude and she could show up at an event at the University of Cambridge and display her nudity, no problem. I never could. Does that make her freer than me? Absolutely! Because it is a pretty fundamental freedom to

[22] Vivienne Rose interview by Wesley R. Bishop, Indianapolis, Indiana, May 20, 2021.
[23] Ibid.
[24] Meredith Ralston, *Slut-Shaming, Whorephobia, and the Unfinished Sexual Revolution* (Toronto: McGill-Queen's University Press, 2021), 183.

feel literally comfortable in your own skin and not feel ashamed of your naked body."[25]

This runs counter to many mainstream beliefs that sees nudity, and therefore human bodies, particularly for marginalized bodies, something to be ashamed of and hidden. Instagram and other social media sites equating sex positive and nudity on par with hate speech, and therefore within bounds to be censored speaks to this, and this view harms efforts to liberate body images and advance the rights of fat people.

Many of the participants expressed skepticism that body neutrality could be used to achieve the need to overcome anti-fat bias. As discussed in the introduction both Alessandra Grima and Carina Shero shared their skepticism, allowing for the area of medicine to be a possible place of "neutrality," but even in that arena both were not sure. Robina Strowder and Jessie Oliver were even more unequivocal, arguing that body neutrality was as much an issue as a watered-down body positivity in lieu of fat liberation.

"I don't know if I can understand how you could make yourself feel neutral about your appearance," Strowder said. "Seems quite difficult."[26] When asked if in the medical profession, and outside of perhaps media representations could body neutrality play a role, Strowder argued, "I actually think that's a funny question. Until the medical profession as a whole can acknowledge and accept that fat bodies can function the same way as smaller bodies, they will never be neutral."[27] The only way to equal treatment would be through a body positive outlook, and specifically a fat liberationist one since it was fat bodies that were pathologized by medicine. That required not embracing neutrality, but a celebration of fat bodies as inherently worthy and needing of care. If as a society we were to simply be neutral then what difference would it make to change bodies from fat to thin, etc. Only by embracing the inherent worth of a diverse set of body sizes and acknowledging how fat bodies were specifically harmed would better services be achieved. Jessie Oliver echoed this sentiment, comparing the push for body neutrality as like the desire of a color-blind liberalism that attempted to ignore race altogether. Fatness is an aspect of human body diversity, and fat people have been discriminated against. To claim, now, a neutral stance was to erase the latter and hope

[25] Ibid., 184–85.
[26] Robina Strowder, online message Wesley R. Bishop, Nov. 27, 2022.
[27] Strowder message, Nov. 27, 2022.

that society simply moved on from its prejudices. It would just drive the issue underground and create a more nefarious anti-fat policy that harmed people of larger bodies.[28]

Embracing bodies, even in the realm of sex and pleasure, was key to many of the participants in their work of creating media of fat bodies. Denying the reality of body dimensions or the reality of how bodies experience pleasure helped no one. As a result, media must reflect this diversity to be fully liberated in its treatment of human body differences.

CONCLUSION

In August 2021, leadership at the social media site OnlyFans announced that beginning in October they would start restricting sex positive and "explicit" content from their platform. This was particularly aimed at sex workers who used the site to run their businesses in a far more safe and transparent manner than they had before. Prior to this site such as Instagram had been deleting and restricting accounts that linked directly to places such as OnlyFans and Patreon. Investors at these sites wanted to go "legitimate" and rake in more money from corporations and advertising dollars. As long as OnlyFans remained a safe place for sex workers, and particularly fat people working in adult entertainment, then that ability to attract that investment would be hampered, so the leadership of the site claimed.[29]

The backlash was swift. Sex workers, activists, and commentators noted that it had been the users themselves who had created the high profile of OnlyFans and now they were being shut out from their own platform they had worked to curate. Fat activists in particular were worried that yet another online space was being closed off to them. Fortunately, the backlash was severe enough that OnlyFans stepped back from their plans to scrub the site of particular users it found offensive for their work and body sizes. Alessandra Grima, reflecting on the affair said she was not surprised. To her this had become a familiar cycle where tech companies would create a platform, sex workers, fat users, disability rights activists, etc. would make the site into a place to work and find community, only to have the

---

[28] Jessie Oliver, online message Wesley R. Bishop, Dec. 9, 2022.

[29] Cheyenne Roundtree and Laura Bradley, "Only Fans Turns Its Back on Sex Workers and They Are Pissed," *Daily Beast*, Aug. 19, 2021. Accessed December 15, 2022. https://www.thedailybeast.com/onlyfans-turns-its-back-on-sex-workers-and-they-are-pissed.

rug pulled out from underneath them when the tech company no longer found it as profitable to tolerate them.

In the last two chapters we will explore how this realization leads to two broad questions, the first in the next chapter will discuss the need for a true public for fat people to exist as fully equal members of society. The final chapter will explore how social media serves as vehicle to push for that, but also represents several issues. But to conclude this chapter, as the participants stated throughout the interviews to make either of those possible (a public and a socially just social media) first society needed to embrace an unequivocal fat-positive outlook in its representations. With this a better understanding of anti-fat bias and the inherent worth of fat people would be far easier to communicate and agitate for in the broader society.

CHAPTER 4

Fatness and the Need for a Public

Abstract This chapter discusses the intersection of fatness and the public sphere, exploring the need for a public to fully realize the aims of body size activism. It also delves more deeply into the concept of republican political economy and how it reinforces anti-fat bias, ableism, and racism in society. Counter to popular belief, it is not solely a corporate or neoliberal political economy that contributes to anti-fat bias. Instead, there is an older assumption about "fitness" and "health" that argues individuals in society must maintain a body size and range of body abilities to be "good" members of a community. This ableism is seen as a requirement of free, democratic societies that supposedly require a healthy citizenry. As this chapter shows, too, much like the criticism of body positivity—specifically that it is personally focused on individual psychological states and allows a privileging of thin to average-size, able-bodied people—fat people need to be able to access the public, be seen and recognized as equal beings in public, and should not through design or social bias be excluded in physical public or online public spaces.

Keywords Fatness • Public • Public sphere • Recognition • Public space • Neoliberalism • Republican political economy • Health • Social media appeals • Burlesque • Tumblr

W. R. Bishop, B. N. Rigakos, *Liberating Fat Bodies*, https://doi.org/10.1007/978-3-031-63890-9_4

Model and activist Saucye West poses for a picture. Her work, like many on Instagram, challenges conceptions of anti-fat bias and anti-black racism

INTRODUCTION

Social scientists and cultural observers often debate the validity of using social media to push for and achieve social change.[1] Critics charge that since social media is a corporate-owned space, the maneuverability of social actors (such as activists and artists) to fully challenge the dominant power structures of our times such as racism, sexism, and capitalism is fatally limited. By now it is clear that the participants we interviewed are

[1] Olivia Guntarik and Victoria Grieve-Williams, eds., *From Sit-ins to #revolutions: Media and the Changing Nature of Protests* (London: Bloomsbury Publishing, 2020).

aware of this tension, and despite the corporate constraints of social media sites the need for a public is central to their body size activism. The repeated sentiment that the act of taking a selfie and posting it for others to see is at odds with critics such as Jia Tolentino and L. Ayu Saraswati who have challenged the practice of selfie taking, posting, and constructing extensions of the self in online spaces.

Both discuss the much-observed phenomena of performing aspects of pain and suffering for an audience, and the shift from "Web 1.0" to "Web 2.0." "What you did on the internet would become intertwined with what everyone else did," Tolentino argued. "And the things other people liked would become the things you would see. Web 2.0 platforms such as Blogger and Myspace made it possible for people who had merely been taking in the sights to start generating their own personalized and constantly changing scenery. As more people began to register their existence digitally, a pastime turned into an imperative: you had to register yourself digitally to exist."[2]

Likewise, Saraswati has argued that the performance of various forms of pain—namely, those around sexual assault and abuse—can and often do follow a logic of neoliberal individualism where the person posting about the issue as it relates to them creates a "neo-liberal selfie" that does not question or address the broader social constructs that permitted the violence. As she explains:

> I also wrote this book to shine a bright, yet troubling light on the pressure to speak up to prove oneself as a feminist/activist on social media. On these digital platforms, silence is too easily stigmatized and equated with complicity in the power structure. Speaking up on social media becomes compulsory for those who need to perform their feminist subjectivity. For instance, during the #MeToo campaign, some other women and I were not ready to share our stories on social media. Yet we felt the pressures to do so and were even stigmatized for being silent.[3]

This follows the trajectory of what some have criticized as the ability of social media sites to convince users to create content not just for self-expression but instead for profit. That is, the content we create as

---

[2] Jia Tolentino, *Trick Mirror: Reflections on Self-Delusion* (New York: Random House, 2020), 6.

[3] L. Ayu Saraswati, *Pain Generation: Social Media, Feminist Activism, and the Neoliberal Selfie* (New York: NYU Press, 2021), 176.

members of these platforms generate free revenue for large corporations that want to gather data on other users searching, staring, clicking, liking, and engaging in comment sections.

There are fair points to all these critiques revealing the troubling aspects of corporate-owned Internet platforms, but as this chapter shows the participants, we interviewed troubled this seemingly easy criticism of online media. Specifically, participants discussed the need for a public, that is a viewing population that saw them as fat people living open, loving, and positive lives. Likewise, the fear that users were simply free laborers making money for corporate companies ignored the fact that many of the participants had, minus the issues of censorship, been able to create sustainable and lucrative work as models, performers, artists, and entertainers. Far from being simple "victims" of social media, the interviews showed that many of them were able to use social media to their advantage, and what they wanted was not protection or a closing of the digital commons but a more accepting digital space to exist, work, and challenge anti-fat biases.

This brings us to the final point of this chapter. The concerns of neoliberalism, although appropriate in many settings, has often been overstated by cultural critics in describing the problems of social media and the digital age. Neoliberalism at its most basic premise operates when institutions and individuals assume that corporate capitalist ideals make for the best social logic in organizing society. What this means is that capital accumulation, the creation of new capitalist value, and private concern of capital over the public common good, are all favored in policies from tax cuts to potential environmental and political impact.

Participants noted that they thought platforms such as Instagram and other social media sites often used a neoliberal logic, particularly in the favoring of large corporate entities over less economically powerful individual users. Yet when discussions deepened to include the contradiction that "fat sells" (either from a corporate body positive angle or from the undeniable fact that fat users gain substantial following on platforms such as Instagram, Patreon, or OnlyFans). Participants argued this continued censorship reflected something more akin to a spirit of Puritanism than corporate capitalism or its political movement, neoliberalism.

There is indeed a type of restrictive conservative cultural logic at play when social media sites actively censor their users based on being fat, sexy, and unashamed of their bodies. Puritanism as a movement harkens back to the sixteenth- and seventeenth-century religious movement that insisted on severe piety, aestheticism, and restrictions to enjoyment of sex, and shame of the body. Puritanism was a factor in the cultural foundation of the United States, but on platforms that actively allow entities like Playboy, and thin celebrities, like Gwyneth Paltrow, to display nude and sexually suggestive content a strict form of Puritanism is obviously not being observed.

It is here that we offer a different explanation based on research from historians who have studied anti-fat bias, political discourse, and socially accepted body ideals. We call this impulse of social media sites to censor marginalized bodies and sexualities, namely fat bodies in this study, "republicanism." What we mean here is social media sites that censor fat bodies often do so from an anti-fat bias that attempts to justify itself through a defense of allegedly "healthy" ideals.

Health itself is a fraught term, full of assumptions, many of which are counterproductive to actual scientific studies, disability rights, and wellness standards of people. But aside from this issue, the bigger question is why is health something that anyone in society, let alone an impersonal social media company, would worry about promoting? The common argument, to which many participants reported being subjected to was the tired line, "You are glorifying obesity."[4] The issue found within this line of thinking is that by promoting what critics see as "unhealthy" body sizes, fat social media users will encourage others to be comfortable with fatness, leading to not only an increase in fat people (something that the United States and other countries have already experienced) but a lack of will to do anything about it. Critics portray this as threat to the public as it, in their reasoning, creates a body of citizens who cannot do certain tasks, cost more to care for, and are a moral failing due to their bodies' connection to perceived greed and excess. The fact that none of this is true demonstrates how much of anti-fat bias is political, not scientific. In this chapter we explore how these issues of need for a public, censorship, and republican ideology. We conclude with an argument, grounded in our participants observations of the need for a better conception of publics, political action, and socially valid actors.

---

[4]Aubrey Gordon, *"You Just Need to Lose Weight" and 19 Other Myths About Fat People* (Boston: Beacon Press, 2023).

PUBLIC SPHERE, SPACE TO BE ACKNOWLEDGED

When we discuss the public sphere, we need to be clear by what we mean. Public sphere can mean anything from media to public space, to the more theoretical models proposed by various social scientists and philosophers. What we mean here when discussing fatness, social media users, and the need for a public is the both the more theoretical aspect of the public sphere as well as the more tangible "space."

The first of these components has been proposed from thinkers like Hannah Arendt to Jurgen Habermas who saw a common need from people to be recognized on some level by mass society.[5] Arendt criticized this component, arguing that such an impulse could create a muddling of private concerns with public matters, whereas Habermas focused more fully on the ability to rationally communicate with one another.[6] Although Habermas and Arendt, as well as their students dismissed the more humane, personal, and allegedly "private" concerns of self-worth, fat liberation and even body positivity shows that such a need to mix private conceptions of the self with the more robust public debate is incredibly necessary.[7] This is so because the problems facing fat people is not merely a personal feeling, nor is it simply a public issue of access. Instead, the inability to access public spaces, employment, or social validation shows how our private conceptions of ourselves are not divorced from our public standing. Bifurcating the two spheres ignores large swaths of social activism, as well as how oppression works both as an internal force of self-hate and regulation to constructing barriers for public life.

Jessie Oliver discussed this when she recounted how she first became aware of body size activism. "I don't know when I first had the words for body positivity, but body positivity or whatever we're going to call being at one with who you are, kind of started when I was younger," she began. "I have a mother who is on the autism spectrum and a father who's a clinical nurse and a sociopath. And I got emancipated when I was sixteen and so I was sort of living in this highly traumatic experience. And there was a moment where in my teenage years I realized there is not enough time or energy to hate myself. Like I am dealing with enough external forces of

---

[5] Jurgen Habermas, *The Structural Transformation of the Public Sphere: An Inquiry into a Category of Bourgeois Society*, trans. Thomas Burger and Frederick Lawrence (Cambridge: MIT Press, 1991).

[6] Hannah Arendt, *The Human Condition* (Chicago: University of Chicago Press, 1958).

[7] Richard Sennett, *The Fall of Public Man* (New York: W.W. Norton & Company, 1976).

problems that me being obsessed with my body can only be ... I only have so much space for that. And this was after recovering from an eating disorder and after it just sort of was like, 'I can't do this.'"[8] Oliver argued that the ability to simply exist in public spaces, fat and unashamed, was paramount to a personal revelation. Aubrey Gordon, too, has written about this in terms of the notorious filming local news organizations will do when running a story about the purported "obesity epidemic." In these clips, news organizations would film, without either the consent or the knowledge of the fat person. Later, the news outlet would edit the film so the person would only appear from the neck down. As authorities spoke about death, suffering, and the danger fatness posed to the public these unwitting fat people, happily going about their lives, would be used as depersonalized representations of public disgust, shame, and ridicule. "That news footage," Gordon explains, "was the most recent in a long line of media portrayals of fat people ... For my whole, short life, bodies like mine had been presented on camera with disdain, disgust, lurid curiosity ... We were set pieces, props to elicit a series of reactions from the more real, thinner people on screen. We weren't people—we were just bodies. Disgusting bodies, funny bodies, pitiable bodies, fearful bodies ... never whole people."[9]

Charlotte Cooper has referred to this phenomenon as the "headless fatty."[10] It represents a clear humiliation and dehumanizing that fat people must navigate when simply appearing in public. It reflects that the basic need of people to exist, unaccosted in public, is a privilege not afforded fat folks, and that appearing in public runs the risk of losing control over one's own human representation. There can be no real public sphere, at least the one idealized by social scientists, as long as this threat continues. The inability to be recognized as a full, and equal person, and not as an expression of a perceived social problem.

Oliver concluded by saying, "... I still have this hardwiring of the shame and guilt my father had very specifically put into me of ... He would tell me I was too fat and ugly to go on vacation with them and then I would wake up and my family had left. Yeah ... My friend Justin Tranter ... was

[8] Oliver interview, Nov. 4, 2019.

[9] Aubrey Gordon, *What We Don't Talk About When We Talk About Fat* (Boston: Beacon Press, 2020), 119.

[10] Charlotte Cooper, *Fat Activism: A Radical Social Movement* (Bristol, Eng.: HammerOn Press, 2016).

in town recently for an award they were receiving and had some of their friends from LA with them and told this story about the first time I ever went out to eat with them. We went to a suburban Pizza Hut and they looked over and realized I was crying and they were like, 'Why are you crying at this Pizza Hut right now?' And I was like, 'This is the first time I've been allowed to eat in public in years.' Like things my father wouldn't let me eat in public with my family because of the shame of having a fat child."[11]

Carina Shero, too, discussed the complications of appearing in public as fat, and the ways that media and space are weaponized against fat people. In one instance she was duped into working with a European film crew to discuss modeling and art. "So, for myself," Carina explained, "I have done a couple of TV appearances and one of those was in Germany, and it was supposed to be a segment on body positivity/body image. But then they actually took the majority of what I said about body positivity out of the final segment and focused instead on how I make money online. Then they sold all the segments they filmed with me to another show without my permission, and so now I am on a show called *Ten Freakiest Bodies*. It has aired multiple times in Germany and Austria, and just two nights ago it was on TV again, which is partially why I think I got deleted from Instagram [this time] because so many people who saw that show reported my account."[12]

Vivienne Rose explained a similar issue in describing how other accounts would repost hers, and content from other fat women, and not be censored by Instagram. "There's the inequality," she explains. Accounts, typically run by men, would gain large followings by reposting the nude images of fat models. Yet these accounts would explicitly state in their bios that they were run by men and that other men should not DM them. This was done in an attempt for the men using other women's work to not receive unsolicited sexual images and messages. "They post stuff that shows it all, and they go unperturbed. And then one of us [fat women] gets censored five times in a row and shut down. And I don't understand

[11] Oliver interview, Nov. 4, 2019.
[12] Wesley Bishop and Carina Shero "Instagram Deleted Her Account @ Over 400K Followers: Fat Phobia in Art and Social Media, and How Carina Shero Continues to Fight for Better Representation of All Bodies," *TERSE*, April 15, 2018. https://tersejournal.com/2018/04/19/instagram-deleted-her-account-over-400k-followers-fat-phobia-in-art-and-social-media-and-how-carina-shero-continues-to-fight-for-better-representation-of-all-bodies/.

that. I don't know how they get under the radar like that. They're posting pictures without our permission for one … So, they're reported for that … They're posting stuff that's not supposed to be on there per community guidelines. So, you report them for that. And they remain up, riding … unperturbed. Never challenged. Successful up to **300,000, 400,000** followers, and I don't get it."[13]

Rose suspected that the issue arose from the fact that men would come to these sites and engage in the same harassment that they did to women's own social media accounts. However, once the harassing men discovered they were sending unsolicited sexual messages and images to other voyeuristic men, the messages would simply stop. This was opposed to women who would ignore the messages and then, in an act of anger and retaliation, their accounts would be reported. "You create this account," Rose explained, "and I understand that it has skin. By nature, there's going to be horniness associated for those who are lesser refined. So, the thirst factor is all the people from the … corners of the internet … who come out and they're like, 'Oh. Female. Sex.' Or, 'I fuck you.' Or just all the comments that are there … The emoticon is … the eggplants of the world."[14]

This means that fat women as commodities of others, be they corporations or just random men using the bodies of women to develop a following out of a shared sexual fetish or attempt to sell a brand, have more freedom in spaces like Instagram and the Metaverse than women themselves. Dignity and control over one's own body, labor, and story in the public square is tenuous at best then in these online spaces.

Public Sphere, Physical Space to Exist

This leads to the second conception of the public sphere, and that is actual space. Physical space has long been a barrier for people with disabilities, different abilities, and different body sizes, yet even in the less physical digital space of online platforms discrimination is easily found.

As will be explored in the next and last chapter, this banning from public platforms has taken even more dire tones with the federal government revisiting laws that governs digital space. Activists and government officials have increasingly challenged the so-called 26 Words that Created the Internet, which prevents social media sites from being sued for content

---

[13] Vivienne Rose interview by Wesley R. Bishop, Indianapolis, Indiana, May 20, 2021.
[14] Ibid.

created and posted by third-party users. Activists in the sex-positive movement, queer liberation, and body size activism are alarmed by this because
it could open the doors to endless litigation from everyone encompassing
transphobic "anti-drag" activists, to overzealous health "experts" who target fat social media users. Likewise, many of these online spaces have, due
to the users in the community, come to serve as an open archive for body
acceptance, sexuality, and sex practice education for scores of people, fat
people included, could suddenly be shut down and destroyed as federal
law removes these speech protections.

Alessandra Grima experienced this in one of the most discouraging and
infuriating ways possible when her account, due to her work as an adult
entertainer and fat activist, was removed. Aside from losing her immediate
list of followers, clientele, and ability to route the viewing public to her
other sites such as OnlyFans and Patreon, she also lost her documented
journey in dealing with a cancer diagnosis and surviving. Grima explained:

> But for months, no one listened to me [about my pain and concern] and
> told me to work out more because my side hurts so bad. And I'm over here
> trying to work out in pain, and I kept going to the doctor and I kept going
> and I told them to give me imaging and I have a severe rare cancer that kills
> people within 12 months. I mean, it's very serious, right? It's very serious …
> It took me 8 months to be diagnosed with a cancer that can kill me in as
> soon as 6 to 12 months. I mean, that sentence alone, it took me three
> months to get an ultrasound. Then they were like, "There's a spot, what-
> ever." And I asked for the MRI and they're like, "Okay, that's nine centime-
> ters." It took a month for me to even see a surgeon. They told me I had
> heartburn and I had to lose weight is what they basically … They were like,
> "Go gluten free." I'm like, "I don't eat gluten, rarely. I like my bread." But
> I went off bread. I had listened to them. But a lot of people look at me and
> assume I eat like shit which even if I did, none of your business, but I did
> take the advice and they were going to do surgery on me without doing a
> biopsy. And I asked for a second opinion. And the second opinion in Boston
> was like, "They didn't test what this is?" She was like, "What are you talking
> about?" And she got me a biopsy and they're like, "Yeah, you have cancer
> and now it's five more centimeters. That's like three centimeters bigger." I
> didn't even have surgery till two months later. But people don't realize, I
> literally would have been dead. I mean, literally, would not be here having
> this conversation with you. And I had nurses that I don't know. I mean,
> multiple nurses at multiple places would read my chart and they're like,
> "Honey, you sent this to this doctor?" They're like, "You asked the doctor
> for the MRI?" They're like, "We've never seen somebody your age even talk

to a doctor like this." And I was like, "It's because I'm not stupid," first of all. Second of all, doctors work for me and it is not the other way around. And thirdly, the sad part is if this happened to me 10 years ago, I'd be dead. I'd be like, "I need to lose weight. I'm too fat." And you can find multiple stories of fat women dying that didn't get listened to.[15]

Once Grima discovered the cancer she decided to document the treatment so that there would be a record and that hopefully others, particularly fat women, would see it and know that they should certainly advocate for themselves. "I've been very open about my journey," Grima said, "because ... I've had multiple DMs like, 'Hey, I asked for a second opinion because you've been posting about your cancer journey.' That's all I care about. I'll always be an open book if it's going to help somebody else. I don't care. Because I don't care what people think about me. Me and my father had cancer, went through chemo, and beat cancer at the same time. He didn't want to tell anybody. And I'm like, 'I'm telling everybody.' That info was going to save somebody's life."[16]

Yet, much of this content was permanently lost when Instagram deactivated the account for allegedly violating its community guidelines. A host of conversations, information, and advocacy was destroyed by a corporation despite being offered freely by a person. It is more infuriating when participants note how uneven this destruction of online space and knowledge are applied:

I've been deleted multiple times ... I'm a nude model, which I can't even write the word nude on Instagram because that's a red flag. Or once I was on live, I was wearing something like this [gestures to clothing] and I was doing tarot. It was actually my tarot account and I got booted for being nude because my cleavage, I guess, is bigger than other people's cleavages, I suppose ... Yeah. So that's why I know they don't like it because I'm targeted, and fat women are targeted, and black fat women are targeted especially, and trans black fat women are targeted even more. And it's like it's very obvious ... So, I have the same amount of followers for almost five years because I'm shadow-banned all the time. And I was shadow banned for maybe three years straight. I would say to 2019, I had just three years straight, it wasn't up and down. And then I changed my gender to male. Someone told me to do that. I was un-banned in the hour. ... Within the

[15] Alessandra Grima Zoom interview by Wesley R. Bishop, May 15, 2023.
[16] Ibid.

hour. Not only was I banned from hashtags or being searchable which is still not, but they erased all of my posts from my own hashtag. So that's how I could tell. Within the hour, I was back like that. … I've been [listed as] "male" since … I mean, I'm sure it'll run [its course] … However, I had male ads for a while. I get them every once in a while, now, but now I'm starting to get more fem ads. I'm like, "Okay. They've probably run that out." But the fact that it worked so fast, I was like, "Come on." I mean, it's kind of sad.[17]

Months later, we followed up with Grima to see how the process was going. It was still infuriatingly opaque. In response, she and many other participants we talked to were forced to create back-up accounts, encourage her followers to follow those too, and hope that both were not deleted simultaneously. Grima admitted that the process of losing her account robbed her of her work as an advocate, artist, and worker, and left her with feelings of depression and discouragement. Was her work not worthy for public viewing? It was a question she easily answered as "yes" but nonetheless the feelings would surface occasionally as she worked to rebuild her online presence.

In the shift from Web 1.0 to 2.0 this need to "perform" or be in a public view to "exist" was something some digital theorists worried about at its inception. Yet the more sinister element of this state of affairs was less the need to perform in a neoliberal logic of "see me, buy me, share me," and more the fact that our online presence is much more of our identity. That identity can be regulated, censored, and when removed it in essence removes "us" from the space totally. It is as much erasure as it is censorship, wiping out an existence as it is expunging a record.

Grima explained that the process of appealing Instagram's decision to delete her was fraught and impossible to fully understand as it was shrouded in vague language on the site's terms, conditions, and procedures. At one point Instagram sent her a link to an external site that could "review" her case and judicate it. She explained she had no idea who these reviewers were, how much information she should share with them, and if it would be secure. In the end she decided not to use the external site and continued to put pressure directly on Instagram. Her reasoning was that she both did not trust an even vaguer process that Instagram conducted at its

---

[17] Grima interview, Nov. 21, 2022.

site, and that the platform's owners and workers needed to deal with the problems of their product, and not outsource it (Fig. 4.1).

Corporate-controlled social media, then, perpetually runs this risk of erasure, but the same could be said about more public, government-based media as well. Aside from discussing issues with social media, participants also described how existing as a fat person in physical public spaces, as either a performer or just everyday person, was equally as important in their work toward fat acceptance.

Vivienne Rose explained this process, detailing how, after she lost several people in her life to untimely deaths, she decided to travel abroad. Arriving in other countries she found that the anti-fat bias, although not exclusive to the United States, was not a universal phenomenon. In fact, many countries vaulted fatness as both attractive and desirable:

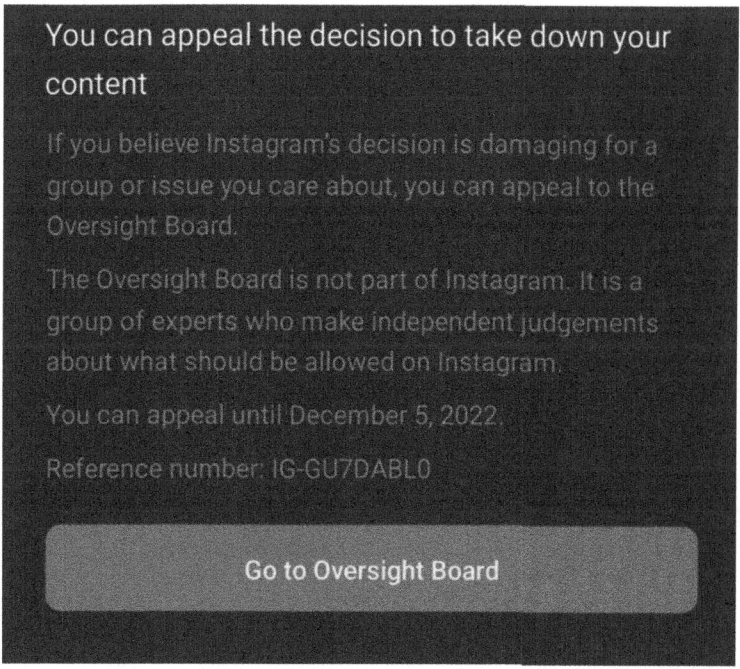

Fig. 4.1 Message Alessandra Grima received from Instagram to challenge her frequent banning and harassment on the social media site

As I traveled, I would go to all these countries. I backpacked for ten months. I would go to all these countries and all these different men from all these different parts of the world were attracted to me ... there was some cross-section of the world that thought I was attractive ... So now, at 43, I would say for the most part I'm almost fully in myself as I am sitting in a space that's sized to me instead of trying to squeeze into a space that I should aim to fit because I was fat which was "my fault" which I should fix in order to fit there. So, I still forget sometimes how far I've come into getting into a scenario where I remember how the old me used to respond. I might post something recently about walking through the mall food court, it's like this ... I don't know. Dead man walking into it. I was like fat girl walking. You have all these eyes, all in this court all in the old days I swore were looking at me and judging me like, "Oh, she's fat." Somewhere along the line, I realized I was pretty self-centered to think that the whole world was worried about me. And even if there was anybody that was looking at me, in about five seconds I was going to walk away from their lives and they were going to walk away from mine and watch that they impact any element of mine. So now that's where I am, but I remember piece by piece, the little improvements that I have made to where I'm almost whole in myself as I am.[18]

Rose's ability to simply exist and limit the shaming voices in her mind was directly tied to the ability to envision and exist in a public space unaccosted by anti-fat sentiment. The point seems clear that as a society we will only overcome anti-fat bias by tying the ability to exist in public as an equal member of society and not a project to "fix" ourselves as a basic right.

Several participants take this idea even further by organizing dance troupes, public shows, and events that required physical public space to do their art. In particular, Carina Shero and Iridessence (Essence Walker) co-founded the Chicago burlesque group *Femme FATales* in 2014.[19]

Shero described the process of founding the group, and how it was a mixture of digital and public space that made it possible:

The idea came in early 2014. I had gone to some burlesque shows in Chicago and I noticed that there was always almost only skinny performers with once in a while plus size performers sprinkled in there. What I noticed is that you could always see the audience's reaction would shift when a plus size performer would come on stage. It would always be this feeling of "Oh,

[18] Rose interview, May 20, 2021.
[19] Nicole Blackwood, "Glitter, Sequins and Liberation," *Chicago Tribune*, July 4, 2019, pp. 4-1-4-4.

is this person going to take off their clothes? Oh … okay." And then there would be this kind of forced applause. And I just thought it was so disheartening because everybody should be championed the same way based on their talents, and not on the size of their body. Especially in burlesque which is a platform that people have used to claim self-expression and empowerment, which to me is part of the broader goal of body positivity. So I was even asked to join a troupe. It was a troupe that had just one other inbetweenie performer, and I had to really think about whether I wanted to put myself in that kind of position where I would have been this afterthought. It would have been this position where my existence was only humored, but not really championed. I wanted to challenge that. I had a lot of professional dance training from when I was in Germany, but nothing specifically in burlesque. So I ended up becoming really good friends with Iridessence, we met through Tumblr, and I told her this idea of wanting to create a plus size burlesque. But I had no idea how to go about doing that. So, it was something we played with, we would talk about it here and there, and then she took me to this ice cream social at Vaudezilla which is one of the main troupes in Chicago. Vaudezilla was created by and is owned by Red Hot Annie who is an international burlesque performer and a star. It was at that meeting that I got to speak to her and pitch the idea, and she said, "You know what? This is really needed. I will support you all in any way." She then provided us space, and reviews, and told us that we had to follow through with the idea. And that was really the fuel that we needed. Two months later we had our first big troupe meeting. We had a lot of people who joined through Tumblr and word of mouth. We ended up with thirteen people in our living room, that were all plus size, and of varying genders.[20]

Iridessence spoke about the founding of the troupe, and how the use of public space was a good step in doing much of this work:

Back in 2014, I met Carina. I met her through Tumblr, and we just started hanging out. We started being friends, and then she was in this program where she was creating a project, like a creative project. Well, yeah. She had wanted to design, not design, but put together a plus-sized burlesque troupe. I'd always had an interest in classic aesthetics and burlesque and

[20] Wesley Bishop and Carina Shero "Instagram Deleted Her Account @ Over 400K Followers: Fat Phobia in Art and Social Media, and How Carina Shero Continues to Fight for Better Representation of All Bodies," *TERSE*, April 15, 2018. https://tersejournal.com/2018/04/19/instagram-deleted-her-account-over-400k-followers-fat-phobia-in-art-and-social-media-and-how-carina-shero-continues-to-fight-for-better-representation-of-all-bodies/.

such at the time. I'd always wanted to do it, but I'd lived in the suburbs up until that year. It was just hard to get out and be able to do it. I finally moved to the city, and I was like, "Oh. Well, I've been here a couple months. I can do burlesque now and figure things out." So we started going to shows and doing research, and then we ended making up a Kickstarter online and getting a couple people who were interested to come by and form a troop. It was a very magical experience. Body positivity and fat positivity, a lot of that happens online. And I think this is one of the biggest issues with people not really getting a lot of the nuances or not really getting enough of what they need out of the movement. It's not having their outside life reflect what they found out online, basically. So, with meeting her and with having a troupe of all plus-sized people, you got to practice being in fat healing spaces in person. That was a really great experience. And then to have everybody going on stage with the express purpose of taking off their clothes and reveal more parts of their body to the audience was a really powerful thing. The audience felt it. We felt it as performers. It's a really fun to be able to do, but I feel like it also provides a service whenever you put fat people on the stage to any people of size in the audience, to be able to see what's that like. That it's a possibility. That it's something that they can do. They can be on a stage. They can be not just the only one on the stage, but they can be a part of a … They can be not the token one on the stage, but they could be the only ones on the stage.[21]

Laura Weetzie Wilson, an early member and co-producer of the troupe, likewise discussed how the work of the Femme FATales had served as not only needed artistic representation for fat bodies, but also a space for fat performers to meet and hold community together:

I've always been a dancer, like my whole life, and it wasn't until I was an adult, and I really wanted to find … Well when I was an adult I really wanted to find another outlet for dance, especially being on stage. And I really loved to burlesque and just always kind of wanted to be a part of it, but didn't know how and under what circumstances. So, through a friend I met Carina [and] Essence and started working on their first show, and at the time I was just a dancer, just a performer. And I put together my first act … and we had the show, and it was amazing and that was real wild and awesome and just very liberating … And then I kind of grew from there with looking at what the troupe needed and what the different members needed in the troupe. I kind of took on a more I guess you could call it like a more executive role,

[21] Essence Walker interview by Wesley R. Bishop, Chicago, Illinois, Nov. 4, 2019.

and yeah, just sort of helping out, producing and figuring things out and kind of directing a little more and putting on shows ever since. What other kinds of things about my joining other do you want to know … Well for me personally, I don't love performing if it's not with my troupe. I know a lot of … I know I could be performing around town a lot more and doing a lot more … But if the space isn't going to be like a fat positive space, I almost don't want to do it. Not because I'm afraid or anything. It's just, I just feel so much more comfortable and happy and that's where I feel free to be myself.[22]

Laura continued by explaining that although one would assume that an art form, like burlesque, with its grounding in feminine bodies, queerness, and celebration of the human body, would be naturally body inclusive the reality was far more disappointing:

I would love to say that it's inherently body positive, but it's not by any means I don't think. I think it's more … I mean comparing to other dance and stripping, it's more body positive just because more bodies are involved and there's less pressure to be a certain type of way, but I don't believe that it's inherently body positive. I think you have to create it and you have to create a space that is going to be acceptable for everybody and I still think there's a lot of room to grow in burlesque in general. I still think it is geared towards thinner bodies and in general and I think that there is a lot of work still to be done just in the community of providing spaces for larger bodies to perform.[23]

Furthermore, she explained, it was in this troupe as well as online that she found actual community to affirm and accept her body type, a thing that was not always present with other groups such as friends and family:

Well, my friends were incredibly supportive [of entering burlesque]. The first time I performed I was actually in Utah and I didn't perform at the Femme FATales. It was like [a] pre-show starting it out, kind of like test of my performance. So, I actually performed in … Utah at a gay club and I performed as a drag performer but a burlesque drag performer. So that wild but it was really, really supportive. Everyone was really great. It was really cool. And then my family doesn't know, my brother probably knows because he knows how to work Instagram, but my parents don't. And I plan on

---

[22] Laura Weetzie Wilson interview by Wesley R. Bishop, Chicago, Illinois, Nov. 4, 2019.
[23] Ibid.

72 W. R. BISHOP AND B. N. RIGAKOS

keeping it that way and they're very conservative and they don't understand and they would be, they're already so disappointed, I don't need to disappoint them anymore. So yeah. But as far as the reaction goes, I think there wasn't a great reaction to the community, to me personally. But I think the truth has created a lot of waves and a lot of visibility. I think as the troupe, I feel like we've established ourselves in the community and have created a space that's unlike any other, where we put on a show that's just ours. And I just really, I don't know. I really love it. Chicago, I wish there was more venues for in Chicago has been kind of hard to find the right venue for us. But I mean as we grow bigger, which I hope we'll always do, hopefully we'll get bigger and bigger venues. Yeah.[24]

Another one of the performers in the troupe, who requested to remain anonymous echoed these sentiments as well. "Carina dragged me into it," the participant joked:

When I moved up to Chicago, I was in a really bad relationship … When I ended that relationship, Essence and Carina invited me to a slumber party here. And they had tried making contact with me prior, but because of that relationship, I was isolated. But they tried again, and they're like, "Let's see if she responds to this invite." So I did. I came out like February of 2017, and I didn't know … I knew them from my Tumblr days and stuff like that, but it's different when you meet someone in person. And I knew that they had a burlesque troupe, and I've always loved burlesque. And Savannah, where I moved from, there's a troupe there that I took classes with, and it's a world that I've always loved. But performing, I didn't really consider it. But when I came here for the slumber party, Carina was like, "You should audition. We just held auditions." And I was like, "I don't know about that." And she just pushed me. She worked on me for like twelve hours … I stayed the night, and we went to an IHOP, and we sat there for like four hours, and she just kept pushing and pushing. And eventually I was just like, "Okay, I cracked. I'll put something together. I'll send it to you guys."[25]

It's a decision that the participants did not regret. Explaining further, they recounted how the work in the troupe had helped not only them but also

---

[24] Ibid.
[25] The participant requested we refer to them only by their stage name and online persona "Dimple Dutchess." Dimple Dutchess interview by Wesley R. Bishop, Chicago, Illinois, Nov. 4, 2019.

audience members feel more positive about their bodies and question why they had been conditioned to hate their body's shape and look:

> That's what does it for me is, one, our last shows sold out. So that means something, right? But every time we go, we get messages that trickle in from people, not just saying that they enjoyed the show and it was awesome, or bad ass, or whatever. We have people that are like, "I actually feel like I'm worth something." They actually take away something transformative within themselves from it. And that's more than you can ever really ask for to be a part of. I remember one of the things I do love about our shows is usually our finale incorporates pulling audience members at the very, very end. And then we'll have a really fun song pop on, and we're all dancing. It becomes like a dance party. And I try and select someone that I feel like I see it in their eyes throughout the show, that they're just like, "I don't want to be there." And they just drag them on, and then you see on their face, and they're like, "Wait, this is happening. You're actually dragging me up onto the stage." And it just becomes this magical ... One woman ... She had brought her husband with her. And it's when things kind of settled and people are just kind of walking up to us, and talking, and hugging, and pictures. She was just like, "Yeah," basically, "I'm feeling myself, and I'm going to get pregnant tonight." So it's overall just the best thing in the world.[26]

The participants reported a mixture of ideas about public space, both digital and physical. They argued that the digital public space was necessary to be seen, to build larger communities, and most importantly to push ideas into more national global audiences. Conversely, they also argued that physical public space shared with like-minded and like-bodied people provided a major benefit of personal body acceptance.

The successes of these artists and activists, to produce and sell tickets to shows, as well as generate online content that people are willing to pay for, raises an important question though. If fat performers, models, or adult entertainers, can be so financially successful, why do platforms continue to censor them? This is even more confusing when the messaging and guidelines from social media platforms is inconsistent.

In the final section of this chapter, we explore this issue of anti-fat bias in a particular form of capitalism.

---

[26] Ibid.

REPUBLICANISM AND THE POLITICAL ANTI-FAT

As we have seen body positivity has the issue of two co-optations. As participants explained, the first is a whitewashing to make body size acceptance more palpable to anti-fat societies, the second is capitalism, and both are linked together. Activists in the fat liberation movement have argued that body positivity often is collapsed into "feel good" for white women, and that this personalized approach privileges mostly thin to average-size white women.

Of course, fat liberationists note that thin to fat white women, as with all sizes and racial identities, should love their bodies, but by turning to a personalized approach the movement loses focus on social issues, and more troubling, does little to address white supremacy.

Likewise, this focus on white femininity acceptance also allows corporate capital to co-opt the movement by simply creating a new market for entities that have long profited from anti-fat bias. New clothing lines, new products, new advertisements, etc. are all adopted by these allegedly progressive corporate brands, and in doing so acceptance of bodies—fat, thin, of various disabilities, etc.—take part in an economic system that is unsustainable and exploitive.

Participants placed different emphasis on this in their responses, with some saying that inclusive items from brands were not only good but a desired goal. However, there were differentiations in what type of consumer goods corporations offered and whether it was truly progressive or not. For example, clothing was a focus of many of the participants' response. For example, Saucye West has focused much of her activism on highlighting which brands have legitimate inclusive fat clothing. Transportation, too, was another focus. Vivienne Rose, in particular, discussed this aspect, explaining that for her work as a model and performer commercial airflights have been a constant source of inaccessibility.

Commercial goods such as razors, soaps, perfumes, etc., although fun, were not all that progressive according to participants. Instead, they were representative of the same previous commodities repackaged and often focused on reactionary politics of exclusive white femininity. Likewise, clothing that corporations purported to be "size inclusive" but in fact was not, was a point of ire from participants throughout the study (Fig. 4.2).

This raises the question of how political economy intersects with anti-fat bias, body size activism, and access to commercial goods. In total participants did not readily provide clear alternatives to capitalism, with some

Fig. 4.2 Saucye West poses in clothing. Part of her work is demonstrating both how fat can be beautiful and modeling clothing brands that claim to be size inclusive

participants mentioning capitalism explicitly as a negative, and arguing for forms of social democracy, socialism, and communism, while others did not mention political economy. When participants did mention political economy, however, there was a critique of capitalism with no one arguing that fat people were economically well served in current capitalist economics.

Asstyn Martin explained this common critique found in the interviews toward capitalism by saying:

[S]o many of those [products and services sold by the diet industry] are unhealthy. Especially the quick weight loss schemes that are out there. They cause damage to people. I mean, I started dieting for the first time when I was, I think the least that I can remember probably eleven, something like that. And I had so many times where I would lose weight, gain weight, lose weight, gain weight, and they've done research and said that really can mess up your metabolism. And so, I feel like it's undoing some of the damage the diet culture has done. And it's mostly the capitalism really … It's all about selling us, they tell ex … making sure that we understand that we're flawed and in order to change and be accepted, we need to buy all of these things to change our appearance. So, it's all driven by that.[27]

Jessie Oliver echoed this sentiment when discussing her work on consciousness-raising with people on the topic of fat liberation:

I also think people can take it upon themselves to educate themselves. There are podcasts, there are books, there are articles that I just wish people read that HuffPost article, "Everything We Know About Obesity Is Wrong," I wish I could just keep that article somewhere for anyone to read at any moment to unpack the fact that insurance companies and diet companies have driven a lot of these numbers and these statistics about bodies historically. And it enlightened them and open their minds about everything you have been programmed about weight is actually incorrect because internalized capitalism leads to internalized fat phobia.[28]

Yet during the interviews a tension arose in discussing the issues of anti-fat bias, capital, and online censorship. There was an undeniable irony in that criticisms of anti-fatness, of capitalism, and that other radical displays of documenting the medical industry, transportation, and legal system would be tolerated by social media sites. But the far more benign, and body spositive approach of simply feeling good about one's body, naked and free of social criticism, was the expression more often censored by social media platforms.

So, although the oppression of anti-fat bias is not an internal force, but an external state, we must contend with the fact that radical criticisms of diet industry, medicine, and transportation are not all that censored on social media sites. Instead, social media sites will censor and punish the far

---

[27] Asstyn Martin Zoom interview by Wesley R. Bishop, June 24, 2021.
[28] Oliver interview.

more benign photo of a fat person in shorts, or naked. As a result, the radical critique is permitted in the capitalist and reactionary space, while the liberal and less radical act is punished.

This signifies that the oppression of fat people is not solely capitalistic, at least of a corporate variety. Corporate capitalism has shown that it can, like many radical and liberal movements before it, re-brand itself in the face of criticism. Of course, this change does not actually alter itself in the immediate to being less exploitative, as participants noted corporate capital carries with it certain exploitative and reactionary assumptions, but from body positivity to fat liberation a purely corporate capitalist logic can easily sidestep the issues we have raised in this book. This is most clearly seen in how if one follows corporate capitalist logic, a practice often referred to as "neoliberalism" in early twenty-first-century online left-wing activist circles.

Yet to collapse anti-fatness into neoliberalism fails to account for why social media sites would not simply want to profit from fat users who generate content, clicks, engagement, and ultimately revenue. Shero discussed this issue when she pointed out in conversation that fat people, even when working in the adult entertainment industry, make a living off their content creation focused on their bodies. So, if as Shero puts it, "fat people sell," why would entities such as Instagram and other sites not want to financially profit from fat users in the same way they do their thin, sexually explicit, and often corporate-backed users?

As body positivity has shown, products can be made, sold, marketed, etc. that incorporate positive displays of fatness. "Oh, there's multiple things," Shero starts. "So, first of all … one thousand percent fat bod[ies] sell. Oh my God. Even if it's not entirely like, "Oh, yay, we're here for this fat body," but fat bodies get sensationalized and that's views, which end up equaling for you being able to sell things."[29] Shero then described an instance when the musical artist Miley Cyrus featured fat model Angelina Duplisea in her videos.

And so, I think about the Miley Cyrus video where she had a bunch of marginalized folks in it, which she totally was exploiting them and fuck Miley Cyrus. I hate her with a passion, but she had … [a model and actress] who was a superfat … and Miley Cyrus on her Instagram had made a post for each one of the people that she was exploiting essentially in her music video.

[29] Carina Shero interview by Wesley R. Bishop, Chicago, Illinois, April 14, 2022.

And so, they were all getting a certain amount of likes and everything like that, right? And the photo of … [Duplisea] by far was getting … wildly more engagement than anybody else's post. It was getting a massive amount of likes and then also a huge amount of comments, which of course, a lot of the comments were incredibly fatphobic, which of course Miley Cyrus did not monitor the comments. She has teams of people she could pay to have monitor these incredibly harmful comments, which there was also a trans person in another post where there was transphobic stuff and that was also not monitored … And the numbers on [those posts] were what we call "doing numbers," right? A huge amount of engagement. And this just happens in general. This is just an example of fat bodies getting a huge amount of engagement, which in capitalism equals dollars, right? More people are watching this video, more people are engaging, right? Yeah. And like I said, photos of me on other people's pages are always doing really well and selling whatever it is that they're trying to sell, lingerie, hair products, whatever the hell it is, right? Anyway, so that's not it. Yeah. I think that there's multiple things at play, one being that Mark Zuckerberg is a douchebag. I mean, he created Facebook as we know for him to rate hot girls. And he just does not think that fat people are hot girls. So, he just in general doesn't want us on there. Majority of his employees at higher level are douche dude bros like that, that just want to have a certain type of body. And for some of them they might want to have a fat person, but they're not going to admit to that, then they're not going to write code to support that, right? Because it's a secret. And so, I think at the first level of the inception of all of these apps is this level of cis straight man that has a very Western European idea of what beauty is and how we should regulate that, right? So, there's that layer. And then I think what I've encountered, and this is a theory, I don't have actual … I've not done a thesis on this, but I very, very strongly believe that in most societies, and especially in American society, people have been taught so deeply to think that fat is the biggest moral failing, that it is the most disgusting thing, that is all the bad things.[30]

Fortunately, there has been quite a bit of research done on this. Most notable is Sabrina Strings' 2019 book *Fearing the Black Body: The Racial Origins of Fat Phobia*, and Da'Shaun L. Harrison's 2021 book *Belly of the Beast: The Politics of Anti-Fatness as Anti-Blackness*.[31] Online activists often use these books as ready citations when educating audiences about the

[30] Ibid.
[31] Sabrina Strings, *Fearing the Black Body: The Racial Origins of Fat Phobia* (New York: NYU Press, 2019). Da'Shaun L. Harrison, *Belly of the Beast: The Politics of Anti-Fatness as Anti-Blackness*, (San Francisco: North Atlantic Books, 2021).

historical roots of anti-fat bias and how it is founded in our current era in anti-black racism. Memes that feature pages and quotes from the books are often circulated, with messages of encouragement for people to buy, read, and discuss the topics in the books.

What Strings' and Harrison's books show is that if we are to understand anti-fatness in the early twenty-first century people must first comprehend that much of our social order owes its hierarchies and practices of dehumanization to a specific global history era called the "Early Modern Era" which lasted from roughly the 1600s to the 1800s, and particularly focused on what historians call "the Atlantic World." This latter term refers to the continents of Africa, Europe, and the Americas and how violent, global transactions shaped what we would call the Modern Period. In this period, European elites invented conceptions of race to justify enslavement of peoples from Africa, removal and murder of Indigenous peoples in the Americas, and forced relocation of a newly created working class in Europe.

Part of that justification was a reimagining of the ideas of beauty and social worth. As scores of historians have documented by the end of this period in the late nineteenth century, white able bodies, were seen as not just a norm but also the only acceptable ones to wield social and political power.

This was an explicit moral argument, and it was a morality that sought to justify both a society of free individuals living off their own labors and independent from monarchies, while also enslaving, subjugating, and eradicating other humans that interfered with the new economic system of global capital. What Strings argues is that during this long period societies, in particular in Europe and North America, argued an "average" human body that was neither too fat nor too thin would be a reflection of a person who could regulate themselves, and therefore be trusted to vote, hold office, and be trusted with civic freedoms in the emerging republics of the early modern era. Black bodies, through much pseudo-science and political propaganda, were associated with either fatness, which signaled an inability to stop intake of resources, or thinness, which was a sign of being weak and unfit for the strains of citizenship.

A political economy emerged from this that valued regulation, balance, and conceptions of an idealized democratic republic above all else. This political economy allowed for powerful criticisms of forces such as monarchism, but too, justified slavery, colonialism, and the exploitation of low-wage workers. If we compare these political economies to one another, we begin to see how a republican political economy fits with anti-fat bias, and how the early twenty-first-century social media sites can be both hyper-capitalist, and profit motivated, while also being explicitly anti-fat. In capitalist political economy, particularly the kind of neoliberal corporate capitalism people often imagine, profit above all is a motivating factor. Scores of academics and activists have criticized this practice as neoliberalism subsumes all human endeavors and landscapes, including the natural environment, into an outlook that sees only potential economic growth as good, and anything that does not produce new capitalist profit as inherently inefficient and therefore "bad." The opposite of this is a social political economy that values use and collective well-being over all else. In this outlook profit for profit's sake is not only seen as irrational, but also offensive and dangerous as it does not see the natural world, or human relations, as anything other than a plan to make more money.

But between these two opposites reside a host of mixed political economies that take various features of both, and in many cases whole other logics. Feudalism of the ancient world is an example of this. The slave economy of antebellum America is another. In both cases neither overall economic profit nor social good was prioritized, and instead a social hierarchy based on birth or race was the main goal of maintenance for the political economy overall. In republican political economy, then, the goal is to maintain a conception of a republic for society. The stakes in republican political economy, then, is nothing short of a loss of a purported "free society" of "independent actors."

Fat people, which is a subset then of people with disabilities, are seen as a direct threat to the maintenance of that republic since in the imaginary of the republican political economy fat people are equated with blackness, which in the context of the United States' earlier eras was equated with the status of slavery, the exact opposite of a free citizen. As slavery was abolished and the United States' various left-wing social movements pushed for greater gender, class, and racial equality, that anti-blackness did not dissipate but instead changed forms from chattel slavery to apartheid Jim Crow laws, to criminalization of Blackness by the current American legal system. From the body of enslaved Black people to Ronald Reagan's vilified "Welfare Queen," the republican political economy insists that fatness is an indicator of political downfall. Children, then, are forced to diet, run a mile, and do a certain number of pushups in gym class. Why? Because the maintenance of a thin, fit body is good for the person, who is only seen as a citizen, who is the building block of the Republic.

That is the morality at play when social media sites censor fat users. When social media platforms target fat users, but then allow promiscuous content from thin users, or powerful economic entities such as *Playboy*, we see this anti-fatness at work.

This brings us to the final point of this book, and that is how social media sites such as Instagram, TikTok, and others are violating basic conceptions of civil liberties that are meant to protect marginalized people from differential treatment by private business entities.

In the final chapter, we will explore the conceptions of freedom of speech, civil rights in online spaces, and whether online spaces have been good for activists in the body size movement.

CHAPTER 5

Social Media as Tool and Hindrance

Abstract This chapter looks more closely at the area of social media, considering how it has been both a tool and a hindrance to the body size activism movement. As participants argued, social media has allowed them to post images of themselves, as they want, and tell stories about their lives that do not need to accommodate anti-fat biases in traditional media. However, this ability to be explicitly pro-fat—as well as sex positive, anti-racist, and activists in various causes—has been hindered by outright censorship (deletion of accounts and content), soft forms of censorship such as shadow banning (where social media companies limit the reach of content without notifying the user), and social media companies platforming and promoting hate groups. The history of Twitter/X is discussed in relation to Elon Musk's acquiring of the company, and various artists and technology advocates are interviewed here who are either part of or adjacent to fat liberation. The chapter delves into the concept of online enclaves, both their power and limitations, and the realm of disability awareness, free speech, and the challenges facing the art community writ large as companies favor certain content while suppressing others.

Keywords Technology • Shadow banning • Algorithms • Platforming • Hate speech • Twitter/X • ADL • New enclaves • Lips.com • Online rights • Free the Nipple

W. R. Bishop, B. N. Rigakos, *Liberating Fat Bodies*,
https://doi.org/10.1007/978-3-031-63890-9_5

Jesse Duquette, sometimes referred to as "the most shadow banned cartoonist on Instagram" discusses the double standards found online when right-wing material is permitted but critiques of the Right, or other topics such as body size activism, are censored

INTRODUCTION

Anti-fatness exists as an intersecting point in a broader web of reactionary politics. Included in this are anti-sex, racism, ableism, homophobia, and transphobias. Participants in the study argued that social media sites can either foster these politics or actively combat them. This argument bears out in research in digital humanities. Cathy O'Neil argues as such in her book *Weapons of Math Destruction*, which explains how algorithms on social media sites present the illusion of choice, while amplifying some users' content and hiding others. "The math-powered applications powering the data economy were based on choices made by fallible human beings," O'Neil explained. "[M]any of these models encoded human prejudice, misunderstanding, and bias into the software systems that increasingly managed our lives. Like gods, these mathematical models were opaque … the model itself is a black box, its contents a fiercely guarded corporate secret…."[1] Ruha Benjamin has demonstrated this issue as well in her study *Race After Technology: Abolitionist Tools for the New Jim Code*. Biases of programmers have been passively, and sometimes even actively, worked into the new technologies of the digital revolution ensuring that the prejudices of human society continue in a new iteration.[2]

Social media platforms have, with the rise of algorithms and other software designs, developed computer programs to help curate content for their sites. These programs encourage the visibility of some content, while "pushing down" other content. The criteria for how this selection is made is not entirely clear, because the algorithms needed to make this process are proprietary knowledge, and therefore privately held secrets. It is a well-established line of argument in technology studies that society, with its inequities and beliefs, cannot be separated from the technologies of that society. Benjamin has referred to this issue as the "anti-Black Box" where the secret algorithms and other technologies of governments and corporations are used to explicitly harm people of color.[3]

During the research for this book this observation emerged as an overarching argument with those we spoke to about the issue of anti-fatness in society. Technologies, be they social media sites to seats on an airplane to metrics such as BMI, were made to marginalize particular types of people consciously or unconsciously. Body size was one of these explicit areas that technologists often targeted for harassment, harm, and silencing.

Social media serving as an ally to extreme right-wing movements is a growing issue for democratic societies. This was most dramatically displayed by the business magnate Elon Musk buying the social media site Twitter in 2022. Musk is a self-proclaimed free-speech absolutist and was critical of Twitter's previous efforts to regulate hate speech and political extremism. Specifically, Twitter had banned Donald J. Trump from its site

---

[1] Cathy O'Neil, *Weapons of Math Destruction: How Bid Data Increases Inequality and Threatens Democracy* (New York: Crown Publishing Group, 2016), 3–8.

[2] Ruha Benjamin, *Race After Technology: Abolitionist Tools for the New Jim Code* (New York: Polity, 2019).

[3] Ibid., 34.

following the January 6 Insurrection attempt by his supporters to overthrow the government and stop the Electoral College from finalizing the 2020 presidential election. Musk maintained, however, that censoring Trump from the site was violation of the spirit of the First Amendment to the US Constitution, bad business, and also unwise as it did not silence Trump, but just kept him from being seen and checked by the wider public. "Banning Trump from Twitter didn't end Trump's voice," Musk stated. "It will amplify it among the right and that is why it's morally wrong and flat out stupid."[4] (Fig. 5.1).

Musk stayed true to his word and reversed the previous decision once he bought the company. However, Musk's conception of free speech did not extend to everyone, and it quickly became apparent that he would, as Twitter's new leader, censor and target users and organizations that were critical of him or his politics. In fall 2023, Musk, then well settled into the leadership of the social media site, began a public feud with the Anti-Defamation League (ADL).

Established in 1913 in Chicago, Illinois, the ADL is dedicated to tracking, prosecuting, and preventing hate crimes, particularly those committed against Jewish people. The ADL, along with other anti-hate, anti-genocide, and civil rights groups had long criticized Musk and other free speech absolutists for platforming extremists that then aided in legislative and extra-judicial acts of violence against marginalized populations.

White nationalists, right-wing extremists, and then Musk himself charged that the ADL was guilty of silencing speech by noting, publicizing, and then criticizing groups that encouraged hate crimes against Jewish people.[5] The argument escalated quickly to Musk threatening legal action,

---

[4] Brian Fung and Clare Duffy, "Elon Musk Says He Would Reverse Twitter's Trump Ban," *CNN Business*, May 10, 2022. Accessed September 9, 2023. https://www.cnn.com/2022/05/10/tech/elon-musk-twitter-trump-ban/index.html.

[5] Yair Rosenberg, "Elon Musk's Latest Target Hits Back," *Atlantic*, Sept. 8, 2023. Accessed September 9, 2023. https://www.theatlantic.com/ideas/archive/2023/09/adl-twitter-jonathan-greenblatt/675258/. It should be noted, too, that the ADL has garnered its own fair share of controversy over censorship efforts. For example following the beginning of the Israel-Hamas War sites such as Wikipedia threatened to downgrade the ADL from a reliable source citing multiple times the organization had falsely labeled stories, information, and sources as 'anti-Semitic' for simply disagreeing with the government of Israel. Likewise, Wikipedia charged that the ADL was publishing false and misleading statements about the conflict. David Goldman, "Wikipedia now labels top Jewish civil rights group as an unreliable source," CNN.com June 20, 2024. https://www.cnn.com/2024/06/19/media/wikipedia-adl/index.html

Fig. 5.1 Jesse Duquette depicts businessman and South African family heir Elon Musk in a caricature criticizing the double standards of "free-speech absolutism" on many social media sites

specifically for defamation, and costing Twitter (by then renamed to "X") for the social media app losing billions of dollars in advertising.[6]

The hypocrisy was not lost on observers. Leadership at Twitter/X was allowing figures and groups with well-known right-wing and extreme agendas to use the global network, but the same leadership was threatening groups that revealed and organized against these very groups.

[6] Margaret Sullivan, "Elon Musk's Hypocrisy about Free Speech Hits New Low," *Guardian*, Sept. 7, 2023. Accessed September 9, 2023. https://www.theguardian.com/commentisfree/2023/sep/07/elon-musks-hypocrisy-about-free-speech-hits-a-new-low.

Alessandra Grima reflected on this issue, saying that as a working-class woman who relied on digital space to make a living, it was infuriating:

> It's like, I can't do anything against billionaire ... what am I supposed to do against a billionaire? ... It's like we have no voice. Every time I try to speak out, I'm deleted. Every time I try to exist, I'm deleted. Not even from a business point, it's as a person I can't enjoy social media. Period. I can't exist here. And I've been told that many times on many platforms. It actually bothers me when people are like, "Why don't you try another platform?" Because they deleted me four times. That's why. I've been trying to use Twitter. Twitter is not an image-based app. Sure. I have an okay following. Maybe it's almost 6,000. I guess that's okay. But it doesn't work the same. It's not as easy. It doesn't look as pretty. Also, I don't think many things will be allowed there much longer.[7]

The future of social media was a concern for several of the participants. They mentioned Meta's policies, Instagram, and also problems at TikTok, Twitter/X, YouTube, and government laws and regulations that would silence particular users on the basis of marginalized identities and shutter swaths of the Internet dedicated to fat liberation, queer education, and sex-positive content.

In the conclusion, we discuss this looming threat of government reach into the digital sphere, yet for this chapter we look specifically at the double standards of social media companies, how communities have fought back individually and collectively, and finally question whether social media has been a tool or a hindrance to body size activism.

What is clear is that the platforming of neo-Nazis by conservative and reactionary figures, like Musk, is also combined with liberal democratic biases that essentialize freedom of speech without analyzing social and political power, harm to marginalized peoples, and how freedom of speech is not automatically extended to people because of body size, ability, sexuality, or race. These populations, with their various political action as on social media and everyday use of the technology are being told by mainstream society and tech companies through censorship that they are unworthy of equal consideration.

The issue of online spaces, that is just online spaces, is how do programmers and users create spaces that both foster human expression and

---

[7]Alessandra Grima interview by Wesley R. Bishop, Providence, Rhode Island, Nov. 21, 2022.

connectivity, while also taking into consideration the world from which social media is created? In the previous chapter, we discussed how participants shared a skepticism that the goal of social justice was even a concern for designers and owners in Silicon Valley. Likewise, we demonstrated in Chaps. 2 and 3 that workplace safety for fat women working online was not a priority of social media sites.

In this chapter, we will explore a final set of questions that looks at social media as tool and hindrance for social movements such as body size activism. Specifically, has social media helped or hindered social movements? What rights should social media sites have to include in their designs?

BOTS SCANNING

Jesse Duquette, sometimes referred to as "the most shadow banned cartoonist on Instagram" is no stranger to online harassment and frequent censorship on sites such as Instagram.[8] Although Duquette has always been interested in art it was not until the 2016 US presidential election that he began to gain widespread attention. "And then the election cycle started to happen," Duquette explains, "I began to do political drawings occasionally ... And then when the election happened, immediately after the election, I was kind of on social media, it was such as depressing environment because everybody that I was connected to or friends with was just obviously crushed, very bleak and feeling really hopeless. And then the other half where people [who] were gleeful in a pretty evil way. And so, it was just kind of a gross place to be in that moment in social media, so I was kind of ... off of it for a little bit."[9]

Duquette remained off the platforms for weeks, until in January 2017, when the Woman's March occurred. His wife, mother, and cousin all went to D.C. to participate:

And so, when that was taking place, I was down at my folks' place in Connecticut with my dad watching it on TV while my wife and mother were down there actually at the rally. And it really struck me the size of that crowd at that point, I think it was probably, maybe still is, the largest gathering I

[8] Jennifer Krasinski, "Goings on about Town: Art, Jesse Duquette," *New Yorker*, May 5–June 8, 2023. https://www.newyorker.com/goings-on-about-town/art/jesse-duquette.

[9] Jesse Duquette Zoom interview by Wesley R. Bishop, May 15, 2023.

think to date. And it was really compelling to see what was organized, but also organic in terms of how widespread it was. Literally every town, whatever town you were in, had their version of that march take place. I thought it was just really pretty incredible.

And then of course, that was happening across the world too, which I thought was really fascinating. And so, I got back on social media and I saw that this energy was something that made people feel for the first time in a couple months at that point, certainly since the election, not that there was a happiness around that, but there was, I think if nothing else, sort of this optimism behind such a huge movement under a single purpose. And around that time exactly is when there was the first press conference and Sean Spicer made the claim about his inauguration being the biggest crowd or whatever it was. And in that moment, I remember just sitting in my parents' kitchen and it just struck me as like okay, well technically this being the first press conference, you could almost say this is day one of the Trump administration. Now it's official, now he's got a press person who's out there giving a statement on behalf of this new president.

And it just struck me as such a crazy, provable lie, and it felt so unnecessary to lie about that of all things. But here we were day one, and if you're going to lie about something that was truly the definition of gaslighting in that moment, what would that mean for day five or day twenty or day one hundred? If this is already how crazy it is, imagine how awful it could get. So, I did a drawing of Sean Spicer, really almost no editorializing. It was really just a pretty straight image of him, drawn of him, took no creative liberties. And I forget the word bubbles, it's like, "Biggest crowd size of all time period," which I think was what he had said. And then paired it with a quote in mind I had that I had just come across recently from 1984, George Orwell quote, paired it at the bottom, and then put it out on Instagram and Facebook. I didn't have a Twitter account yet, so I just put it on those two with a caption that said something along the lines of, "Day one of this administration, I'm going to do it every day until it's over, until it ends in handcuffs or calamity."[10]

Duquette continued with this practice of drawing/reporting on the news of the day, specifically the doings of the Trump administration for the four years the forty-fifth president was in office. Duquette explained there were days that due to the high number of incidents from the White House he would draw two, three, sometimes four or five cartoons in a single day. By the end of the administration, he had amassed a large archive

---

[10] Jesse Duquette, interviewed by the author, via Zoom call, May 15, 2023.

of artwork. However, as Duquette's work grew, and along with it his following, he found increasing issues with censorship, right-wing trolls, and explicit threats. At about the time of the Unite the Right Rally in Virginia (August 2017), Duquette learned about Instagram's ability to automatically scan photos and censor them on the basis of their content, either by removal completely of a post or by shadow banning it in searches:

I've gotten many, many, many posts taken down. Sometimes there will be a reason ... but just as many times, if not more so, really there's no clear sense of what it is, what the offending component to the drawing is. But it started happening ... right around the Unite the Right Rally [in] Charlottesville. And if I'm not mistaken at that point in time, I had used swastika imagery and some drawings when documenting the Unite the Right Rally. And I think some drawings got taken down because there is apparently some kind ... of an AI function that will scan posts for particular imagery, one of which being the swastika, right? So, the idea being that it'll flag those and take them down. And I understand fully if you're looking at that kind of a system, they can't read for satire, they can't read for irony, they can't see context....

Now, I would accept that if that was true, but ... I came across an account, someone shared with me [of] some random guy somewhere who was posting this really hateful, antisemitic stuff. And the first post I saw was he had hung an effigy of Bernie Sanders out of his window with a Star of David on its chest and hanging. And then the post immediately before or after that was just a swastika. The entire post was just a swastika. I reported both of those images and they stayed up. And this is just one example ... [so the community standards are] not universally applied at all. And I think that's my main problem with all of it is the amount of posts that I have that are taken down that are devoid of anything truly offensive really. I mean I think my work may be caustic in tone, but I don't know that it's offensive necessarily. But the amount of it that gets taken down without any recourse, and I usually will try to plead, and it'll never put it back up. And yet other things that are just unquestioningly boldly and proudly racist, antisemitic, misogynist stay up 100% of the time. So, it's not evenly applied. And to me, that's the main problem. You're either going to have a community guideline or you're not.

Duquette is far from the only person to have this issue with poorly defined standards that are applied unevenly, much to the detriment of regular users as well as voices critical of hate groups. In June 2019, representatives with the Adult Performance Artist Guild, a formally recognized labor union that represents sex workers in the adult film industry, met with leaders at Facebook to discuss the many issues that workers were facing in terms of censorship, harassment, and unfair application of online community standards.

During the meeting, representatives from the union asked specifically if the company was using programs, or "bots," to automatically scan images, measure the amount of skin being shown, and then deciding if an image was pornographic or simply nude on that basis. The representatives did not hesitate to answer and said point blankly that they did. Karina Newton, one of the leaders of the Public Policy hosting team stated, "We have one billion users worldwide. We do use machine learning to proactively try and identify content that is likely violating. Yes, you could say the machine learning identifies 'percentage of skin,' though the reality is a bit more nuance and complicated."[11] The executives meeting with APAG, according to the story, offered very few details on these nuances and evaded several of the more specific points, except when the question of women's nipples were discussed:

> "Are nipples allowed?" asked APAG member Michelle Montana.
> "No." The negative was said in unison by all members of the Instagram team. The clearest response during the entire meeting.
> [An APAG representative] brought up mainstream influencers and celebrities posting pictures with mesh shirts and transparent fabric.
> "Well, if there's an attempt to cover," explained [another Facebook representative], "we consider that as 'non-violating nudity.'"[12]

The executives then stated that, "It may feel inconsistent. But it's not. I assure you."[13] This assurance has been seriously questioned, not just by the participants interviewed for this book, but in wider fields of general observation by commentators who note how consistently inconsistent the standards around women's nipples being censored are on social media sites. When pressed on this, the executives stated that it was perhaps a difference in defining art versus porn, and that was simply a subjective issue.

---

[11] APAG, "Instagram Policy Team Meets With APAG, Listens to Adult Performers' Concerns," APAG blog, June 21, 2019, accessed January 5, 2023. https://apagunion.com/2019/06/21/instagram-policy-team-meets-with-apag-listens-to-adult-performers-concerns/.

[12] Ibid.

[13] Ibid.

In 2008, women held a "nurse-in" at Facebook's headquarters to protest the censoring of women's bodies. Likewise, thousands of women planned to change their profile pictures to that of them breastfeeding or images from famous works of art showing the same action.[14] In 2021, the "Free the Nipple" movement mobilized again after Instagram removed artist Pedro Almodovar's poster for the new film *Madres Paralelas*. The poster depicted a lactating nipple and was flagged by Instagram as violating its community standards. Backlash led to Instagram formally apologizing and allowing some of the images to return to the site. Yet, the hashtag #FreeTheNipple was censored in the site's search functions.[15]

These issues relate to not just anti-fat bias, but also a more widespread reactionary position to women's bodies, sex, and people who work in the adult industry. Yet, all these concerns were expressed by fat people on social media and specifically in the interviews conducted for this book. Arguing that these reactionary politics hurt fat people as well, participants explained that policies such as using bots to scan for skin shown as a percentage is an immediate concern for fat people on social media. And it stands to reason. If a thin person posts an image of themselves in a tank top and shorts, then they will be showing less skin, than if a fat person, wearing the same outfit, posts a picture of themselves. In fact, if the bot only looks for skin and body size, then a thin person could, very easily be posting images that are near nude, or nude implied and not be flagged. This is in comparison to a fat person who could even be much more conservatively dressed and still censored.

What this shows is that the bias of programmers who fail to see fat people as worthy of being in public and enjoying the same rights as thin people, gets written into the technology policing social media. Executives arguing there is no bias, and that when they favor rich celebrities such as Gwyneth Paltrow, Miley Rae Cyrus, Kim Kardashian, and Lizzo to show whatever they want, while punishing working class sex workers or everyday users who are fat, that such a concern is really of no consequence to them. Again, the right to simply exist in public is hindered, and an entire group of humanity is significantly barred from the digital commons.

[14] Sue Dremann, "Nursing Moms Protest Facebook Censorship," in Palo Alto Online, Dec. 29, 2008. Accessed January 5, 2023. https://www.paloaltoonline.com/news/2008/12/29/nursing-moms-protest-facebook-censorship.
[15] Emma Shapiro, "Free the Nipple: A History of a Hidden Movement," *Hyperallergic*, Oct. 5, 2021. Accessed January 5, 2023. https://hyperallergic.com/681937/free-the-nipple-a-history-of-a-hidden-movement/.

These policies also do considerable damage for efforts in the LGBTQ community. Models such as Ady Del Valle, a fat gay male model, discussed in interviews how he has repeatedly faced censorship for his larger chest. Often misgendered, or incorrectly labeled as a woman or transwoman, Del Valle and fat models like him have had to repeatedly fight against stereotypes of what queer men can look like.[16] Furthermore, when the issue of censorship does apply to gender queer and transgender people, many members of the trans community have discussed how having images of trans bodies removed does a huge disservice to the LGBTQ community. The ability of queer people to post images of their bodies, unapologetically and in ways that are flattering and affirming, helps educate queer folk who are first coming to terms with their identities.

One participant we interviewed, Audrey Grison, echoed this sentiment as well. A French artist and disability activist, Grison uses a wheelchair for mobility. In 2016 she decided to try modeling, and then again in 2021. The ability to pose for images, use her body to make beautiful art, and then to share it with a wider public was a major step in not just embracing her own body but also helping diversify notions of human beauty:

[I]n 2016 I went to Paris and there's a group of photographers on Instagram … And they were doing a worldwide tour, and they were in Paris. I was like, "Great, I want to do it." And it was not so expensive, so I was like, I'll try it. But it was my first time, and I was like, oh, my God, am I going to look ridiculous, or whatever? And I had the best time. It was just so much fun, so crazy. I had to change and to be in a tail in front of the Eiffel Tower. It was very insane. And, I don't know, it was fun. But then I didn't do much after that. And in 2021, in the middle of the pandemic, I had a lot of anxiety and I need to find something to do. Which was like, okay, I need to get out of my home. I need to have fun. And so, I went and called a friend of a friend, she's a Colombian … and she's in Toulouse. And so, we went in the countryside and in colza fields, and we made the picture. And when I saw the result I like, oh my God, it's great. And it was the first time I thought, okay, maybe I can make something out of it. Maybe, I don't know. And each time I was doing a photo shoot, what I liked the most is a process

---

[16] Spencer Icasiano, "This Boston Artist Protests Social Media Censors and Celebrates Photographing Nipples," *WBUR.org*, Aug. 2, 2019. Accessed January 5, 2024. https://www.wbur.org/news/2019/08/02/ally-schmaling-instagram-censorship-nipples. E. J. Dickson, "Why Did Instagram Confuse These Ads Featuring LGBTQ People for Escort Ads?" *Rolling Stone*, July 11, 2019. Accessed January 5, 2024. https://www.rollingstone.com/culture/culture-features/instagram-transgender-sex-workers-857667/.

of creativity right before the shooting. Which is like, okay, I have this idea, I want to do this. What do you think? Okay, make it. Just the communication, exchange. Which is like, I just love to make something in my head to make it real. It just so exciting. And so all of this is quite selfish because what I think is that I did [it] for me, but at the same time it's quite selfless because it just made an impact on [how] all people picture disability ... And then I'm like, okay, if I can make something so different, so strange for some, make it look good or look normal, or look creative and sexy, or whatever. Then I'm like, okay, I've done my job.[17]

Grison, despite reporting overwhelming positive feedback, went on to mention that her initial thought was that she would offend viewers because they would reject seeing someone with disabilities posing and posting pictures of themselves. Grison stressed that the majority of the feedback was not that, but the threat of negative comments was still a concern, particularly given past experiences with ableism in the non-digital world.

This ties into what Carina Shero stated earlier in the chapter about failures at content moderation by social media sites. Although social media sites are not directly responsible for the messages of hate another user can employ, the extent to which these companies have gone to negatively impact fat users, for example, while allowing verbal abuse is frustrating for many users.

The Internet could, in short, serve be one of the greatest tools of documenting and educating the general public on queerness that humans have ever invented. But that is only possible if social media sites remove their programming, and divorce their technology from biases against fat, queer, and other marginalized peoples.[18]

Finally, a question must be raised: Why, if these social media sites will censor and empower so many reactionary voices, do they continue to censor so many fat and sex-positive voices? If the goal, as these companies state, is to protect people, then why allow right-wing extremists?

One argument is that social media sites are primarily interested in profit as a business. As unfortunate as it is, right-wing extreme content does generate profits, both from the engagement from left-wing users and from sympathetic reactionary users as well.

---

[17] Audrey Grison, "Interview with Audrey Grison: Disability, Art, and the Self," by Wesley R. Bishop, *North Meridian Review* Volume 4: Issue 1 (Fall 2023): pp. 136–152.
[18] Alexa Tsoulis-Reay, *Finding Normal: Sex, Love, and Taboo in Our Hyperconnected World* (New York: St. Martin's Press, 2021).

Yet in the last chapter we have seen the issues of this argument. Social media sites have been more than eager to censor fat users even though it cuts into their overall profits. To simply allow fat users to have their corner of online space as an unaccosted enclave would be good for profit and would also allow the sites to argue for a true neutrality to their content curation. Yet that is not the case. Instagram, for instance, openly states that it curates its content to create a more "welcoming" environment that is "safer." So, the question is, why the double standard?

Jesse Duquette attempted to answer this:

> Your guess is as good as mine. I really don't know. I mean people will jump to the conclusion like, "Oh, because they're run by right wing people." And yes, they're run by right wing typically, I mean that's just kind of how it's played out, but I don't know that I could know enough about these organizations to know who the mods are or the admins, go through this stuff. I really don't know. And I am a little lukewarm to think like, "Oh, it's infiltrated by a bunch of MAGA hat-wearing." I mean, to me that feels a little paranoid, but at the same time … What's the explanation? Why would those two things, how could those coexist given what they tell us are the community guidelines?
>
> So, I really don't know. I don't know how you could, if you're someone who's tasked with being some kind of moderator for a site like this, and someone reports a page or a post that's just a swastika, to flag that, to come across it and then determine like, "No, that's good," I mean I really don't know. One person had, when this had come up at some point, made some kind of comment around the lines of the notion that in the social media world, people who work in these industries, there's this sort of bifurcation where you're either for free speech and against cancel culture, or you're against free speech and you're for cancel culture. And you find people in these social media worlds who obviously land squarely in the former camp, and so there's this pretty black and white delineation with no gray area like, "Okay, well, if you're attacking what they would qualify as free speech," that's a red flag where I'm like nope, that's way worse.
>
> And like you mentioned earlier referencing Facebook free speech absolutists, I think the close I've come to getting sort of a general sense or idea what it could be, it's that overgeneralization maybe, but of this allergy I think some people have when you begin to talk about curtailing some of the truly offensive stuff out there, some people, the red flags go up and like, "Oh, you're trying to censor. You're trying to inhibit free speech, you're looking to cancel." And so I think there's this oftentimes just over-distortion

against the forces who are trying to call out that hateful speech when you see it....

I would say the one I've noticed the biggest change with is Twitter and truly, honestly, very much as soon as Elon took over, my feed is 100% different. So that's the thing where it's felt definitely the most intentional in terms of, "We are going to really curate this platform in a very different way. We're going to push to you what we think we really value." To me, it's the most obvious. I mean if I didn't know about the change in leadership, I would definitely notice that something was majorly different because it's a complete change from what it had been before.

In terms of the other platforms, I don't know. I think I've seen over time the changes have been more in terms I guess I would say demographically, a little bit of content. Facebook has continued to skew older. Instagram, when I was first starting this [cartoon] project, was I think still at that point still in its essence of being a vehicle mainly image-based, just image-based content. That was really the thing that was driving all the content. And now I think it feels like so much more ad-driven content. Not that I ever spend a ton of time scrolling on these platforms, but it does feel like ... I guess I felt on all three of these platforms that over the past year or so especially, everything feels more aggressively curated. They're really trying to introduce something to you, or they really will push something heavily.[19]

Carina Shero was more explicit in her answer:

Yeah. I think that there's multiple things at play, one being that Mark Zuckerberg is a douchebag. I mean, he created Facebook as we know for him to rate hot girls. And he just does not think that fat people are hot girls. So, he just in general doesn't want us on there. Majority of his employees at higher levels are douche dude bros like that, that just want to have a certain type of body. And for some of them they might want to have a fat person, but they're not going to admit to that, then they're not going to write code to support that, right? Because it's a secret. And so, I think at the first level of the inception of all of these apps is this level of cis, straight man that has a very Western European idea of what beauty is and how we should regulate that....[20]

This ultimately raises the question of what to do about these issues. Participants have engaged in a host of online and in-person activism.

[19] Duquette interview, May 15, 2023.
[20] Shero interview, April 14, 2022.

Carina Shero and Alessandra Grima have, like the Free the Nipple campaigns, led protests outside of Instagram's New York headquarters. Users
have raised these issues online, sometimes leading campaigns to encourage
others to collectively launch complaints to the appeals process on social
media, as well as attend when CEOs of these companies hold "town hall"–
like events and direct other users to come as well and fill comment sections
with complaints to demand action from social media companies.

The results have been mixed. Some in-person events are well attended,
while others are not. Carina Shero, for her efforts, was eventually able to
get an account, after multiple deletions, secured with the coveted "blue
check." Yet, in the following months, this achievement meant far less
when Musk at Twitter/X began selling such markers to anyone who had
the money and willingness to pay for it. The effect has been to lessen the
importance of this status on multiple platforms. Also, she was warned that
this status could be revoked whenever Meta wanted. Alessandra Grima,
too, was able to recover one of her accounts, but again, this was only after
much fighting. Other fat, and sex-positive users have also benefitted from
the activism, with brief periods on social media sites being less militant in
censoring. But all of this still is based on the fact that companies and their
executives can discriminate against users, on virtually any basis, at a
moment's notice.

In response to this some artists, programmers, and activists sought to
create alternatives to the social media giants. The creators of these platforms have presented them as alternative online enclaves that are body
size, queer, disability, and sex-positive conscious. However, these new sites
posed significant hurdles as we found out.

NEW ENCLAVES

The issues of censorship from Meta, specifically Instagram but also
Facebook, has led a number of activists, academics, and artists to try and
create new online enclaves that are accepting of different bodies, explicitly
pro-sex, and who do not stigmatize workers in the adult industry. Two of
these creators are Val Elefante and Annie Brown. Together, the two
founded an app called Lips in December 2020.

Prior to this, Lips had been a 'zine on college campuses on the east
coast of the United States. In 2007, Brown had created the concept as
part of a final project for her gender studies course.

"So, Lips was founded as a pre zine on William and Mary's campus." Elefante explains. "This was Annie Brown, my co-founder … [she] started a 'zine and invited folks on campus to submit their art expressions of, so body, sexuality, really anything from poetry, to photography, the drawings, to a magazine that she'd cut and pasted together and made into Lips zine. So that's the origin, it grew, people on campus really loved it, it was felt like a safer, better place to express oneself … [Lips was founded as a counter to the big fashion magazines of that time]… like *Cosmopolitan* magazine was a big thing back then. And that was kind of like, her response to that, seeing all the same types of skinny white straight women all the time on the magazine covers and stuff…."[21]

Brown explained more, "I went into women's studies class, and we learned about the male gaze, and that really helped me understand. I think we did an activity that was like, "Name the favorite part of your body," and I put my stomach because it was flat and I got compliments on it. But then the teacher said, "Why didn't you put your legs for helping you to walk around the room or your brain for helping you to function or your hands for helping you to do the work that you enjoy or the art that you enjoy?" And it's like, "Wow, that's a really interesting point. Why did I automatically put my favorite part of my body as the body part that I thought that people viewed positively?"[22]

Neither Brown nor Elefante is fat, but instead fit within the range of "average" and "thin" by American social standards. Yet both spoke about the issues of either seeing friends and family struggle with disordered eating or experiencing it themselves. Both discussed the issues inherent in body positivity, but both argued that the act of celebrating, accepting, and defying body standards was a major issue for them. Brown continued:

So, that same women's studies class we were asked to do a project and address a problem on campus, and so the problem I saw on campus was twofold, one, that I felt that the only resource that women and just anybody on our campus had for talking or for learning about sex and sexuality and body image and just that that whole umbrella … because I think for me, body image issues really fit in with sexuality issues, because a lot of mine was like, "Oh, I have to look a certain way to get a sexual partner." And so, it brought in the two, and I think for me it was more about how they both fell under this mental health and self-expression. So, basically, we created Lips as

[21] Val Elefante Zoom interview by Wesley R. Bishop, April 4, 2022.
[22] Annie Brown Zoom interview by Wesley R. Bishop, Sept. 29, 2021.

a zine as an alternative to traditional women's magazines that were basically promoting this male gaze and promoting sexuality from the White male straight cis perspective and ask people to put in their own entries and just express themselves about sexuality, about their bodies, sort of a similar model to PostSecret but being more focused saying really like, "What do you want to say that's going to make you feel better about yourself and something that you want to share with others?"

By 2010 Lips zines had spread to other university campuses. The idea remained the same— create publications of text and images that combated the male gaze and was queer, sex-positive, and body-size inclusive. These campuses included Duke University, Virginia Commonwealth University, Appalachian State University, and the University of Mary Washington. There were even rumblings of chapters beginning further north on campuses such as NYU. Word of the 'zine largely spread organically through writer, artist, academic, and activist circles. "People learned about it, because we had this physical zine," Brown remembers, "and I think people would take it to other campuses visiting friends, and then they would talk about it and say, "Yo, cool, I want to do something here." Every chapter took very different forms. Appalachian State, they did the traditional print zine, I believe at Mary Washington too, they made a print zine. Then at some of the other campuses, they actually turned it into like a Tumblr, so they didn't have a print version, but they would have monthly meetings where they would discuss feminist, queer theory, Black Studies issues in their group, and then move towards collecting submissions and publishing those on their Tumblr. So, every group was very different, but it was the same idea of creating a space for open and honest expression, not only for the members of the group, but for the whole campus."[23]

By 2019, Brown and now Elefante began looking to take the concept more into the digital sphere. Elefante, who was a student at Harvard University, had learned about *Lips* as it expanded out into other campuses. Her academic work looked at queer sex and sex positivity. Through various student groups, including the tour guide group on campus, she had developed a circle of activist friends and colleagues to push for more sex positivity in mainstream understanding:

[23] Ibid.

I was involved in Sex Week at Harvard. And I was in one of the most sex positive, body positive, I would say social group, but we were also the tour guiding group. And it's interesting because that group, I don't know there's different perceptions of what that group is. And we like most other kind of clubs at Harvard, it's exclusive and in some extent, but that is how all of Harvard is. That's a whole other story, but everyone in that group, and kind of what it's known for, as tour guides, is that it like is intentionally very diverse. And very queer, I think there's something about the energy of that group that's very queer and very sex positive, like there's a lot of kind of safe space rhetoric and celebratory rhetoric that I think kind of gets to some of these movements as just like, being in your body and expressing yourself as a radical act. That was the group where I felt like I could do that most and best and kind of finally felt like a safe space for myself, I would say out of more so than any other group I've ever been a part of. And then things like advocating with Sex Week at Harvard for safer sex and being part of those workshops and things being put on around campus was kind of the way that my activism or kind of stepping into a leadership role in these realms manifested.[24]

Brown explains that the move to online formats was a natural one. Many campuses had already begun to do so, and, since launching Lips there had "been a shift obviously from people getting information about sex and sexuality and the ideal body type from these consumer magazines, shifting to now social media." Brown stated, "And so I think Lips fits really well in that because just as we interrupted that narrative of this male gaze of magazines, we're interrupting that narrative of the male cis gaze for the internet."[25]

In the 2010s the venture moved first to a website called lipszine.com. "That was before the Instagram," Elefante explained. "We don't know what happened to that, it basically stopped working. And it was on Amazon Web Services. And we had just at that point, spent hours upon hours trying to get it back and no technician could get it to work. So, we're not sure what happened. It could have been censorship, it could have been, I don't know, some type of technical difficulty...."[26]

As a result, Lips moved to Instagram, and then launched its own app in December 2020. Elefante explained further, "Lips ... evolved into an

---

[24] Elefante interview, April 4, 2022.
[25] Brown interview, Sept. 29, 2021.
[26] Elefante interview, April 4, 2022.

Instagram account, and grew and started interacting with the artists that were submitting to the 'zine and [started talking more directly with] other types of leaders across sex work communities, feminist activists, fat models and activists, queer sex educators, queer activists, black activists...."[27] But the growth of the community came with backlash. "Like there was a lot of, there always is a lot of censorship of, just like racial justice movements in digital space. So, seeing all these different communities affected by kind of oppression and silencing of their voices, Lips became a home for many, and grew on social media." The app/zine became one of the many responses to Meta's handling of content and censoring of some users. "And at the same time started getting censored by social media, which was exactly what the whole thing was founded to solve for. And so, Annie went and crowdfunded for the first version of the app itself."[28]

However, the issue of censorship proved to be an ongoing issue for Lips and other alternative online communities. Many of these new online enclaves hoped to replicate the widespread use that Meta and Twitter/X had, at least in part, so that as many people could come and express themselves and see actual human diversity in a safe and supporting space. Yet, the sites were hindered by shadow banning, and outright removal of content. In the process of writing this book, we personally saw this several times when, in attempting to contact someone through a direct messenger app or would tell colleagues about various apps the mere mention of an alternative platform like Lips would result in Meta refusing to send our messages.

The result was that although Lips gained well over 20,000 users in the first six months of its launch, it was stymied. Other sites have faced similar challenges speaking to the joint issue of monopoly and censorship to communicate in alternative spaces, and link to existing platforms.

As of the end of 2023, Lips, Bluesky, Mastodon, and other sites are still in existence, with varying levels of success and use. Likewise, after being initially banned by Twitter, former president Donald Trump launched Truth Social, a conservative and pro-Trump platform that is very similar to Twitter and Mastodon in its features.[29] This has raised the question of

---

[27] Ibid.
[28] Ibid.
[29] Nell Clark, "Trump's Social Media Site Hits the App Store a Year after He Was Banned from Twitter," npr.com, Feb. 22, 2022. Accessed January 6, 2024. https://www.npr.org/2022/02/22/1082243094/trumps-social-media-app-launches-year-after-twitter-ban.

how successful these smaller enclaves can be, as they represent subsections of broader society (Lips for left-wing users, Truth Social for reactionary users, etc.). Although there are benefits to this, there are limits, particularly as it relates to broader social activism. An enclave by its definition is often a place of safety and similarity where people can be affirmed, but this limits the ability to enact change on a broader scale, and it resembles the same issue mentioned at the beginning of this book between fat liberation and body positivity. It is important for people to find themselves in supportive communities, to challenge the way they have been taught to think about themselves and their bodies when those thoughts are negative and anti-fat. Yet, at some point that radical work on the self must be applied to a broader social sphere if it is going to engage with oppressive social practices. As such, the broader commercialized social media platforms are not an afterthought, but like in public seating, transportation, employment, medicine, and clothing, the ability to exist digitally, to not be erased from an entire sphere of human activity, is a basic necessity. In short, fat people and all users when they engage in activities like social media need a public (Fig. 5.2).

FROM A RIGHT TO THE PUBLIC TO ONLINE RIGHTS

"Fat" is not a feeling that needs to be overcome. Participants in this study regularly argued that although they had much to unlearn when they began to embrace their bodies, they rejected the idea that you could "feel fat." By centering fatness as a feeling—that is something to feel better about— we ignore the root of the issue. Even if someone feels good about their body, that does not change the problem of accessibility. Clothing. Seating. Medical care. Employment. These are practices that oppress folks as social factors. Anti-fatness is not a simple psychological issue. It is a violation of basic human dignity, civil rights, and requires systemic, social change to alleviate.

The body size activism approach of using platforms to share images that challenge traditional aesthetics requires a public. It requires that others view the fat body as not just a thing of beauty, but also a person, collapsing the mind-body duality, forcing us to see that the body as an expression of lived human experience both is diverse and deserves dignity, respect, and rights. Yet that only happens with a public. Without someone to see the act of fat and beauty and human life, then the act of taking a selfie, unapologetically fat, becomes a private affair. It may help us individually, but it

Fig. 5.2   Vivienne Rose poses with a sculpture in public, comparing her body to fine art seen every day

does not help as much with the collective. As such, the censorship of fat bodies on social media sites is an attack not just on the person being censored, but an entire movement. It is the further denial of basic civil rights and democratic norms for a whole group of humans.

One of the ways that social media sites have possibly violated the rights of fat users is in a conspiracy to do harm financially to individuals on the basis of their body size. As has been discussed in this book, the definitive proof showing that social media sites purposefully censor is difficult to produce due to the fact that much of the technology is proprietary and not openly shared. This has led academics such as Cathy O'Neill and Rutha Benjamin to "open the black box" of algorithms, shadow banning, and other content moderation tools to third-party boards of experts and government officials to ensure equal treatment is being provided to all users of US-based companies.[30] This would ensure that if there were violations of consumer rights, in particular as it relates to violations of civil liberties, the issue could be flagged and appropriate measures taken to stop the offense.

Grey Johnson, a Washington D.C. photographer and artist who relies on Meta and other social media sites for his work spoke on this issue:

I think [I made the jump to] Instagram ... in 2014, somewhere around that time. Yeah. And at that time when I started Instagram, I had just gotten out of ... some of my art classes and stuff. And I was drawing, and I was painting and I had a friend tell me about Instagram and I was like, "Yeah, yeah, whatever, whatever." So officially I said, "All right, you've been following long enough. Just put something up there, anything up there." And I put a few of ... my artworks up there, some of my paintings and stuff like that, I posted on there. And I did that for like maybe a year or two. And then I took a workshop on photography. It was a fine art nude workshop on photography. I took that.

And again, I was so nervous because I was considering, it's like, "Oh my God." I was thinking about putting some of the photos from that workshop on there and I was completely, totally nervous about it. And eventually I said, "Okay, just do it, just bite the bullet, just do it." And I put it up there and I got a lot of positive responses from it, which blew me away because I wasn't expecting that at all. I was not expecting to have that many positive comments, a lot of it was like, "Oh," I really felt like my work wasn't good enough. And the first few photos that I put up there, I got nothing but love from it. So, it was very exciting.

Yeah. I remember the first photo I actually had taken down was probably a year, year and a half after I started posting my photographs. At that time, it was a little bit more liberal with which you post now—[Instagram] has definitely got a lot more restrictive. But I posted a model, she was in a profile a side view and her nipple was exposed. I didn't even realize that her nipple was exposed. And I came back, and I was like, "Why did they take my photo down?" And so, I looked, and I was like, "Oh," I was like, "Really?"

---

[30] Cathy O'Neil, *Weapons of Math Destruction: How Bid Data Increases Inequality and Threatens Democracy* (New York: Crown Publishing Group, 2016). Ruha Benjamin, *Race After Technology: Abolitionist Tools for the New Jim Code* (New York: Polity, 2019).

And then you could barely see, it was like a little peak of a nipple that was there. And so that was the very first time that I had it removed or one of my photos taken down.

Since that time, I've had photos taken down. I don't have a justification. I literally do not have a justification. I followed the guidelines. I don't show any full frontal nudity. A lot of my stuff that I show is implied. I'll blur the nipples out. I'll blur the crotch out, nothing that I show or shoot or that I post is intended is sexual. It's like an overtly sexual manner or overtly sexual nature. And I've had stuff recently [removed] for sexual solicitation, which blew my mind because I'm like, "There's nothing." And I've noticed other photographers and other body positive accounts will have the same thing done. Their photos will be taken down for sexual solicitation. So, it's like, they're no longer targeting nudity. Now they're trying to imply their sexual solicitation.[31]

Johnson continued explaining that after having his account suspended and his activities limited (he could not post or share content), that he had to repeatedly plead his case to Meta. "When my photos had gotten taken down, [my account] was disabled. I had to reapply for it and basically plead my case and say, 'Look, I do not sell pornography. I'm not a pornographer. I'm an artist. This is what the intent of my account is.' And I told them, I was like, it's a fine-art nude account. I follow the guidelines. I'm not asking anybody to send me money. This is my platform. And the account that I have is very similar to a lot of other accounts that are out there … What I'm doing is the intent behind it is to be artistic."[32]

Johnson, who is an independent Black artist, reflected further, discussing the frustration with the hypocrisy of targeting his work, while allowing accounts such as Playboy post similar and more revealing photos for commercial profit:

Oh, it makes you feel slighted. Because by no fault with your own, you're not doing anything wrong. You're following the guidelines, you're following the rules, but you're not given the opportunity to express equality or fairly, or not even in this case, if they're showing full nudity, they're breaking the rules, but they can still do it. Whereas you're following the rule and you're being penalized for it. You're being overwatched for it. Again, it goes back to an expectation that, "Okay, well you're going to do something bad." So therefore, we need to keep our eye and focus on you.' And so it's

[31] Grey Johnson Zoom interview by Wesley R. Bishop, May 27, 2022.
[32] Ibid.

very frustrating because it goes against what it is that you're trying to do. It goes against why you're trying to create. You should have that freedom to express and I'm all about fairness.

If you're going to call it, call it both ways down the middle, just so that we can all be on the same page and move forward. Don't single certain people out and try to hold them to another standard because whatever reason that you may have, whatever bias that you may have, don't single people out and try to hold them to a different standard versus somebody else is going to be a little bit more popular. So that's what's really frustrating about it ... Yeah, absolutely [there's a double standard]. Absolutely ... Kim Kardashian, Gwyneth Paltrow, Playboy. Playboy's going to pay [Instagram] the money. The Kardashians ... and Paltrow, they're going to give you all the followers that Playboy ... or whoever can sell to. So, they have a market, they give you more people that allows them to sell. So that's why they're allowed to get away with stuff that most people wouldn't be able to. So that's definitely the hypocrisy behind it. And that is a double standard, absolutely.[33]

Johnson explained that to be a photographer who worked with models, and since he did not discriminate on the basis of body size and did do nude photos that shadow banning had become a common feature of his online existences:

I think I am currently shadow banned now or had just gotten off another shadow ban. It's something that will happen to me seasonally. I'll say about once a season, a photo will be removed. And then typically when the photo's removed, then you have to go through a few weeks. I don't know if it's like two months or like a month process, but when you try to look your name up, you can't find it unless you spell it out specifically your handle, what your Instagram handle is. Once you spell it out specifically, then you're able to find it. But yeah, I've been shadow banned. I've had tons of friends who are models that I've been shadow banned. It's just something that just, after a while you just get used to it ... [and with] shadow banning [what happens] is your content is not being displayed. You're not going to be on the main list. I don't know a whole lot about how the algorithm of Instagram works, but let's say Joe's shoes starts up their Instagram handle and you can look up Joe's shoes or it'll show up on the ... on the [main] feed, but if your shadow banned, then you're not going to show up on the feed. You will not show up [on] anybody's feed. The only way that you can be discovered is if

[33] Ibid.

somebody actually types in the entire name of your handle. ... And so [its] is like [being on] probation, they restrict what it is or what that account can do. They deny it and say that it doesn't exist. But the reality is that it's there and everybody knows that it's there so.[34]

The fact that this leads to a loss of revenue for artists is not lost on people this has happened to. One such user, who did not want to speak on the record for fear of future retaliation from Meta, began a longer legal campaign and social action against Meta when their Instagram account was removed. Posting pictures of themselves that had been removed alongside similar images from Gwyneth Paltrow, Kim Kardashian, and Playboy, the individual made the argument that conspiracy to do economic harm was being carried out by the company, and that Meta's behaviors raised issues of monopoly and unfair practices for users and consumers. Fortunately for the individual, Instagram capitulated rather quickly and reinstated their account, but the issue remains a major hurdle for individuals who do not have the legal connections or knowledge to effectively threaten these powerful companies.

The rights of these independent artists, then, are often ignored and treated unequally compared to the content moderation of large companies and rich influencers. Johnson, and other participants we interviewed, do not simply have the choice of leaving large platform social media companies and choosing to exist only in smaller online enclaves or non-digitally altogether. To do so limits their ability to sell and showcase their work, as well as learn and grow with other artists in their community. Finally, art and activism are in some ways creative acts that require a public viewing audience. Yes, art can be created to be private and not displayed, but working as an artist, or creating art for social change does not exist solely as a dialogue between the creation and the artist. Others, outside of the immediate self, need to be able to see these works if they are to have a more effective social impact and to be viewed by potential galleries, buyers, and leaders in the arts industry. Participants consistently stated that shadow banning, and outright censorship negatively impacted their ability to make a living as an artist, leading to loss of income. When compared to how large companies can, through economic clout, be exempted from the same rules applied to harm fat, people of color, and independent women artists it is easy to see the case that some of the participants raise about

---

[34] Ibid.

conspiracy to do harm and violation of basic rights to equal service by a company.

Alessandra Grima discussed this in some depth when discussing the possibility of online enclaves. To her, although the smaller platforms offered the ability to create safe-haven communities of similar people, it did little to help her as a fat independent artist. Furthermore, she was skeptical that such an approach would be beneficial in the long run. She cited the cases of OnlyFans and other sites turning on their fat, people of color, and sex work users after the platform became more mainstream.

For Grima, the issue was one of a drastically unequal fight. Individuals like herself could not take on multi-billion-dollar corporations, their billionaire owners, and do so on a platform they totally controlled:

> Unless the masses decide to let fat people and sex workers and marginalized groups, I don't think we're getting anywhere. I don't know what that looks like, because sure, I could start small and, in my state, to try to get some sort of something going to change Internet laws. But is that on the top of the list? Probably not. Right? Sometimes I'm like, who gives a shit what happens to me? Why would fat people be on the top of the list here?[35]

Grima continued and explained that although the prospects were small at getting legislatures to pay attention to the concerns of online sex workers and fat people, it would have to be the realm of the law, specifically civil rights protections, that would lead to change:

> [These concerns] sounds silly, but it's our lives now. And that's what I think people don't understand. Because when we were [protesting] outside of Instagram, me and Carina, a lot of old white men were like, who gives a shit about social media? It's like people are killing themselves because of social media. That's why. Because everybody needs it. Because every business needs it. Because everybody's on it. So, you can pretend it doesn't matter all you want, but it does. End of story. Also, I'm just speaking from my place as a fat person who does online sex work, but it's all intersectionality. I'm speaking because that's what I'm living. But the same things are happening to people of color, to trans people. Every marginalized group. When I'm speaking from my place, the same if not worse, is happening to many of us. When I talk about being silenced because I'm fat, I am in a way echoing

---

[35] Alessandra Grima interview by Wesley R. Bishop, Providence, Rhode Island, Nov. 21, 2022.

everybody else's. It's the same problem. … I think making it better comes down to law. And that's why I'm like, we can only do so much. I'm not a lawyer. I'm not a millionaire. It kind of ends there. You know what I'm saying? … Unless I meet a lawyer millionaire tomorrow who specializes in social media, I don't think anything's going to get better. It's funny because it took a decade for me to build a safe space on my Instagram to the point where I didn't see hate speech anymore, or you're a fat bitch, or whatever. Now that I have to start all over, that's all I get. I'm like, oh, I forgot this existed. I just started my Reddit, and I already have twenty DMs. "Suck my dick, here's my cock," here's the whole thing. And I'm like, Ooh, I don't miss this. That's what starting social media is like for a woman or a femme person. That's what social media is [currently].[36]

Laws that are similar to the civil rights protections guaranteed to patrons in the non-digital world—namely, the right to services and employment—are required to make large social media companies respect all types of people, regardless of body size, race, or work. And, most importantly, these laws according to the participants needed to be geared to protecting the marginalized, not empowering the already privileged. To many of the participants the opposite of what they desired has taken hold, where right-wing, racist, misogynistic, and large capitalist entities have been given expanded liberties while marginalized people are disadvantaged:

Instagram [in 2019] was like, it's impossible for us to police certain words … [but if they're] policing sex workers, why aren't [they] policing racism and hate speech and violence? And they're like, that's impossible. Meanwhile, the tag curvy is banned. You know what? I'm like, you [Meta] do it all the time. Just not for the n-word. But curvy was really, I mean, literally the proof is in the pudding. A sex worker is more threatening to [Meta] than [hate] groups that will threaten lives.[37]

So far, the efforts of the government have, in the opinions of many of the participants, not helped, but actually have hurt efforts to combat these issues. As we will see in the last chapter, the realm of social media and civil rights protections has much in the need of further progress.

36 Ibid.
37 Ibid.

CHAPTER 6

The 26 Words That Created the Internet and the Future of Online Art and Activism

Abstract This chapter concludes the study and examines some of the recent Supreme Court cases dealing with online content, freedom of speech, and censorship. It provides a brief history of the American regulatory body, the Federal Communications Commission (FCC), and the legislation that the US has used to govern online spaces as a media landscape. This chapter argues that despite multiple iterations of these laws and policies, lawmakers have consistently failed to listen to many marginalized groups, and instead have focused on bolstering or suppressing political speech they find troublesome. These efforts have been couched in rhetoric of safeguarding children from sexually explicit material and predators, but as the participants note, the laws have not done this. This chapter concludes with an analysis of the early 2010–2020s debates around what constitutes "free speech" and how fat liberation figures into these discussions.

Keywords The 26 Words that Created the Internet • FOSTA • SESTA • Free speech • EARN IT Act • FCC • CDA

© The Author(s), under exclusive license to Springer Nature   111
Switzerland AG 2024
W. R. Bishop, B. N. Rigakos, *Liberating Fat Bodies*,
https://doi.org/10.1007/978-3-031-63890-9_6

Carina Shero's photos often draw comparisons to Renaissance and other art pieces, depicting fat bodies at ease, and in comfort

Introduction

First passed in April 2018, the "Allow States and Victims to Fight Online Sex Trafficking Act" (FOSTA) was billed by its sponsors in Congress to be a vital tool to stop the trade of illegal pornography involving minors, as well as stop the solicitation of sexual services in online environments. Its counterpart, "Stop Enabling Sex Traffickers Act" (SESTA) was a similar measure in the US Senate. The bills, signed by then President Trump received the unusual distinction of being bipartisan during a four-year period of deep partisan divisions. On the surface, for many in the mainstream it seemed that the bills were necessary steps to combat sex trafficking.

However, free speech groups and social media users who were already facing hurdles in terms of censorship were alarmed. The definitions of sex trafficking and prostitution could be applied broadly, targeting anyone in the adult entertainment industry. Likewise, the law was feared by LGBTQ activists who saw the efforts to regulate sexual content in online spaces as including educational materials for queer people, particular adolescents who were beginning to explore their terms with their gender identity and sexuality.[1]

"Yeah. So FOSTA-SESTA was supposed to be a law that would crack down on sex trafficking and specifically child sex trafficking," Carina Shero explained. "But what it actually did was it closed down the avenues of the investigators that actually are trying to catch the people that are facilitating these child sex trafficking rings, or just in general are trafficking people."[2] Critics have charged that due to the federal government shutting down avenues where these traffickers had been working independent investigators, non-federal authorities, and advocacy groups can no longer easily track and report these crimes. "[So] because the access that these investigators had was these internet forums like back pages, those kind of things where people were advertising. … But once FOSTA-SESTA became into effect, and even before it went into effect, because a lot of the larger platform started acting as if FOSTA-SESTA was already in place just to be able to not get shut down once it did pass. So, they started banning any kind of sex work, which consensual sex work is very different from trafficking. But in the eyes of these platforms, there is no difference. So, they shut down all the access that consenting sex workers had to advertise their

---

[1] Melissa Gira Grant, "The Real Story of the Bipartisan Anti-Sex Trafficking Bill that Failed Miserably on Its Own Terms," *New Republic*, June 23, 2021. Accessed January 7, 2024. https://newrepublic.com/article/162823/sex-trafficking-sex-work-sesta-fosta.

Aja Romano, "A New Law Intended to Curb Sex Trafficking Threatens the Future of the Internet as We Know It," Vox.com, July 2, 2018. Accessed January 7, 2024. https://www.vox.com/culture/2018/4/13/17172762/fosta-sesta-backpage-230-internet-freedom.

Heidi Tripp, "All Sex Workers Deserve Protection: How FOSTA/SESTA Overlooks Consensual Sex Workers in an Attempt to Protect Sex Trafficking Victims," *Penn State Law Review*, 124 (no. 1, 2019), https://elibrary.law.psu.edu/pslr/vol124/iss1/6.

[2] Carina Shero interviewed by Wesley R. Bishop, Chicago, Illinois, Apr. 14, 2022.

services to be able to vet clients and all these things and make their work a lot safer. So that's one thing that happened, but then obviously the people that were trafficking, their access to marketing in a sense was also taken away. And so, these investigators now have much less opportunity to actually go after these people and find them. So, they actually had [an] adverse effect. So FOSTA-SESTA did not actually help a bunch of people not get trafficked."[3]

Critics such as sex workers, LGBTQ activists, and people such as Shero have argued that in reality the law was part of a wider effort of certain politicians in the federal government to combat advances in the sexual revolution as well as being honest about their own sexuality in an open format. In 2020, Republican South Carolina Senator Lindsey Graham introduced further legislation called the "Eliminating Abusive and Rampant Neglect of Interactive Technologies Act" (EARN IT Act). This legislation proposed a drastic change to laws governing communication industries, and would establish a federal panel to oversee an evolving document that would be a best practices legal guide for social media platforms and other websites. It also allowed for the ability of states to bring lawsuits to internet content providers who did not act on censoring and removing content found to be in violation of the law. Some commentators, particularly groups wanting more action on child trafficking, praised the proposed legislation. However, many civil liberties groups raised alarm that the designs of the bill made it too easy to create a partisan entity that would not only harm sex workers but also penalize political opponents for speech the panel did not want shared:[4]

> So FOSTA-SESTA passed, right? And it changed how privacy works on the internet for certain groups of people and on certain sites within certain margins essentially. The EARN IT bill if it passes is going to essentially revolutionize the way that the internet works, the way that privacy is viewed. There

---

[3] Ibid.
[4] Riana Pfefferkorn, "The EARN IT Act is Back, and It's More Dangerous than Ever," Stanford Law School, Center for Inter and Society, Feb. 4, 2022. Accessed January 7, 2024. https://cyberlaw.stanford.edu/blog/2022/02/earn-it-act-back-and-it%E2%80%99s-more-dangerous-ever. Kate Ruane, "The EARN It Act is a Disaster for Online Speech and Privacy, Especially for the LGBTQ and Sex Worker Communities," ACLU.org, June 30, 2020. Accessed January 7, 2024. https://www.aclu.org/news/free-speech/the-earn-it-act-is-a-disaster-for-online-speech-and-privacy-especially-for-the-lgbtq-and-sex-worker-communities.

won't be any more end-to-end encryption for anything. It'll be a disaster. It's going to end the internet the way that we think of it. They tried to pass it in 2020, which did not work out because a lot of platforms do have an issue with not having any privacy on their platforms essentially, but they've slightly rewritten it and it's come back ... And so, it essentially is just going to make platforms liable for any kind of communication that happens. And for instance, 2020, when all of the protests were happening and everything like that, we were organizing through, like for instance, an app called Signal, because WhatsApp is owned by Facebook. And Facebook, Instagram, and WhatsApp, because of FOSTA-SESTA they don't care about your privacy. They will read your messages. And so most organizers realized, "Okay, well, we have to be able to communicate through a way where nobody can access our communication," which was Signal. So, for instance, on the EARN IT Act, there would be no more privacy on Signal. And so, this would be a huge blow to ... Again, it's not actually going to crack down on child sex trafficking and on sex trafficking the way that it is supposed to, because again, the access is being revoked to the actual investigators that are investigating this, but it would then also take away organizers freedom to organize essentially without being monitored. And then it would really, really in a huge harmful way target sex workers and also queer people. And so, the way that we think of the internet right now is they're technically a freedom of speech, right? We technically can talk about whatever you want and organize and do all of those things, but under EARN IT, that would just not be a reality anymore. And I mean, right now on Instagram, there's so many keywords that are banned and it would be that 10 times. On Instagram if I use the word censored, censorship, anything surrounding the words like algorithm, all of those things, my posts will get pushed lower in the algorithm or they'll just magically disappear. And so I literally can't even talk about the censorship on the app. Now, if the EARN IT Act would pass for instance, whatever the platform thinks is sexual, they're going to ban. So you probably wouldn't be able to talk about, "Oh, I'm coming out. I'm demisexual, I'm coming out." Well, that's a sexual thing that you're talking about. That would no longer be allowed because maybe you're soliciting sex by saying that you're demisexual and whatever, because everything to them, anything that's even remotely sexual, they then deem as sexual solicitation. And that has to go because then they can be liable for this "solicitation," which it obviously isn't. For instance, on Instagram, they read your messages. If you have in your messages like, "Hey, let's meet up for coffee." The phrase "meet up," you can be deemed a sex worker. They can take your entire account down for that. They will not give you your account back.

As of this writing, the bill still has not been passed despite being introduced to Congress on now three occasions. But this does not mean that many platforms have not increased their efforts to censor people and groups previously targeted for censorship. Shero explained further:

[On] Instagram right now, I think that they're gearing up for potential passing of the EARN IT Act because they in the last month have started taking down just people left and right that are … Fat liberationists that are posting fat bodies that are more in the nude, right? It's implied nude. It's not fully nude or anything like that. Porn stars that are fat, people that are doing any art projects around implied nudity around larger bodies and everything like that, everybody's getting taken down right now. I've had in the last couple weeks, I think 25 to 30 posts removed, which then I contested and then they're like, "Yeah, oops, I guess it doesn't violate our community standards." And I'm like, "Okay, but why …" And they're photos from 2017, all of them. I'm like, "What is happening? What are you guys doing?" So basically, every day I wake up and I'm like, "This might be the day my account's gone." London Andrews lost her main account. Sofia Rose lost her main account.[5] So many big name people that are a huge part of also this wave of fat liberation and what then birth the body positive community. And of course, all these thin white women that are able-bodied and are like, "Oh, look at my too low skin rolls," they're getting to stay up. But then the people that actually did the real labor to start this movement that really have been out here are getting deleted. And for a lot of people, that's their livelihood. For London, she runs a sanctuary and she's like, "I don't know how to pay to keep my animals alive anymore because my platform is gone. That was my access to income." I mean, for myself, I'm perpetually poor because I can't promote any of my sites. I can't promote my actual work. I can't post the work that I'm actually passionate about. I just a couple weeks ago for the first time in Chicago had a photo of myself in a gallery, a photo that I shot of myself, self-portrait but it's my butt and I'm not wearing clothes. And so, it's like, "Well, I can't really post this, but this is a huge moment for me. I'm really excited that I got to do that, but I can't even post about it." But I see thin white able-bodied, CIS people constantly half naked. Chelsea Handler

---

[5] London Andrews and Sofia Rose are both fat liberation, naturist, and sex-positive activists and artists on social media. Sofia Rose, specifically, has been noted for her success in the adult film industry, as an example of more diverse bodies (in particular, fat people) being seen by audiences.

Tiffany Lo, "I'm an adult star—trolls call me fat but I'm healthier than people half my size," *Daily Star*, July 4, 2023. Accessed January 7, 2024. https://www.dailystar.co.uk/real-life/im-adult-star-trolls-call-30383921.

has full nipples out and everything and that's celebrated. Kim K is constantly basically naked, and those people don't need that for their survival. They already are millionaires. They don't need their social media, but we actually do. My biggest goal in life is to be a mom, but if I'm perpetually poor, I don't find it responsible for the way my life is set up because I'm also not able-bodied. So, it's going to take more for me to be able to make this happen. And I keep having to put that dream on hold because it's always something with my social media platforms. And the thing is that I'm not able-bodied so I can't work a gem pop job. Sex work and the work that I do within fat liberation, actually is what should be able to pay my bills. Before FOSTA-SESTA passed, I was making a good amount of money. Yeah, I wasn't rich or anything like that, but I was paying my bills and then I had a little bit on the side to travel, do some fun stuff here and there, right? And that's all I'm asking for. I don't want to be rich or anything like that because eat the rich, fuck that. But I just want to have enough to be able to provide for one child and myself and just survive and not every day be like, "Is this the day that I'm essentially losing access to my job, to my community, to my network, to all the photographers that I want to shoot with?" When people think of, "Oh, it's a platform. It's just a platform." No, it's not. It's your community. It's your access to so many new things. And nowadays it's social capital. It's so many things and I already can't get any brand sponsorships or anything like that because they take one look at my work and they're like, "Well, you're a sex worker, so bye."[6]

THE 26 WORDS THAT CREATED THE INTERNET

These efforts to regulate content, people, and speech online are wrapped a 100-year attempt by the US federal government to monitor and police communications and media. First, the Communications Act of 1934 established what is now the governing body of much of American media by creating the Federal Communications Commission (FCC). Largely ignored by many as just another bureaucratic entity in the federal government, the body became much more significant to political debates in the early 2000s with the issue of net neutrality. At the heart of that discussion was whether individuals had a guarantee to equal access and speed for the Internet, or if large corporate entities could buy exclusive rights to being the more accessible avenues of the Internet. The discussion around this has gone back and forth depending on different presidential administrations (the FCC's five members are appointed by the president of the

[6]Carina Shero interviewed by Wesley R. Bishop, Chicago, Illinois, Apr. 14, 2022.

United States and confirmed by the Senate). However, the issue has raised the problem of how large corporate entities can close access to the digital sphere through their economic clout.

Second, the Communications Decency Act of 1996 (CDA) established one of the first real efforts of the US government to regulate pornographic materials on the internet. The bill was part of a widespread effort to curb sexual materials, in particular as it related to anyone under the age of eighteen accessing those materials.

Both the FCC and the CDA have been criticized by free speech advocates since their passage, but it is important to see how the efforts of FOSTA/SESTA and EARN IT exist in a longer legacy of censoring acts, people, and art that is deemed "obscene or indecent."

That said, the CDA did contain one important amendment, Section 230, that some observers have said should be credited with "creating the Internet" insofar as it became a place of free expression.[7]

The section of the law states specifically:

> No provider or user of an interactive computer service shall be treated as the publisher or speaker of any information provided by another information content provider.[8]

This protection allowed for the rise of social media sites because it effectively shielded sites from being held legally responsible for hosting users' content. If a user of social media advocated or engaged in illegal activity law enforcement could pursue criminal charges against that user as an individual or organization doing the activity. But sites such as YouTube, Meta, Twitter/X, etc. would not be held accountable.

The result was that social media sites could more easily embrace a free speech approach because they would not need to worry about lawsuits and criminal charges against them for allowing users more range in their posting.

The issue with this, as we have explored, is that for many people who are fat or are marginalized in some fashion, the internet has never been a truly free and open space. But Section 230 at least pointed to a possibility

---

[7] Jeff Kosseff, *The Twenty-Six Words that Created the Internet* (New York: Cornell University Press, 2019).

[8] U.S. Congress. House. Senate Committee on Commerce, Science, and Transportation. *Communication Decency Act.* 104th Cong., 2nd sess., Senate. 314. https://www.congress.gov/bill/104th-congress/senate-bill/314.

that a freer and more open internet, and therefore public domain, could be possible.

However, the law has come under increasing attack in recent years. In the summer of 2023 the US Supreme Court heard two cases that could have potentially gutted Section 230, and led to increased censorship online. The cases, *Gonzalez v. Google LLC* and *Twitter, Inc. v. Taamneh*, both dealt with the question of whether social media companies could be held responsible for hosting materials used by terrorist organizations, in particular if the content was encouraging or educating on methods to commit terrorism, and if the content was suggested by the social media site's algorithm. The argument raised questions over the legal responsibility of companies that were not merely hosting materials, but also suggesting materials to users as well.[9]

In both cases, the Supreme Court ruled in favor of the social media sites, thereby adverting the larger issue of whether companies would need to drastically shutter many of their users' ability to create and post content for fear of lawsuits.

As such, the situation continues where social media sites largely determine their own content moderation, applying community standards in a fashion that they see fit, with little regulation or oversite. Although participants in this work expressed a desire for more legal protections, they stated they understood, too, that the history of the legislation did not look promising. To date, although certain provisions have been made for free speech, little protection has been given to marginalized users, and the censorship of fat bodies on social media sites continue.

CONCLUSION

During the years of 2016–2020, a debate in American cultural politics took place over the appropriateness of aiding right-wing extremist groups to share their message to broader audiences. From American universities to social media the question of whether to "platform" a speaker who advocated genocide, racism, or regressive politics on the question of civil

---

[9] Adam Liptak, "Supreme Court Won't Hold Tech Companies Liable for User Posts," *New York Times*, May 18, 2023. Accessed January 8, 2024. https://www.nytimes.com/2023/05/18/us/politics/supreme-court-google-twitter-230.html?auth=login-google1tap&login=google1tap.

rights occupied protesters, administrators, students and faculty, as well as the broader digital sphere in social media.

Organizations, such as the free speech absolutist group Foundation for Individual Rights and Expression (FIRE) and cultural critics such as Jonathan Haidt, discussed that attempts by left-wing students and groups to censor or "cancel" conservative to fascist events were engaging in a dangerous practice of normalizing censorship, as well as weakening their own mental resolve to hear distressing ideas. This model of free speech followed the analogy of the "canary in the coal mine."

This argument stated that although racist ideas, fascist individuals, and calls for rolling back civil rights may be repugnant, these figures and their ideas represented a test to see how strong free speech was in a society. If, the reasoning went, a fascist or reactionary conservative could be tolerated, then nearly any other group could also be tolerated. The broadest definition of free speech permitted a flowering for all to exchange in what commentators referred to as "the free market of ideas." Some of the most extreme figures associated with this debate were the American neo-Nazi Richard Spencer and the British right-wing commentator Milo Yiannopoulos. Attempts by different entities inside and outside American educational institutions to bring them to speak on campuses sparked backlash from student groups who protested their inclusion and argued that universities and media outlets could potentially legitimize these extreme voices by airing their ideas continuously.[10]

These discussions of hate speech and the realms of free speech will continue, however it is interesting to note that at the same time period many commentators were fixated on the rights of white supremacists, arguing their freedom of speech was linked to a broader society's ability to remain free, fat people, particularly fat femmes were facing massive censorship in social media and that this was a continuation of a stigmatization going back centuries. The common criticism these fat artists, models, and everyday social media users received was the same that they had heard their entire lives. They should be ashamed of who they were, they should limit their speech and public behaviors, they should, in effect, censor

---

[10] Greg Lukianoff and Jonathan Haidt, *The Coddling of the American Mind: How Good Intentions and Bad Ideas are Setting Up a Generation for Failure* (New York: Penguin Books, 2019).

Sean Stevens, "Canaries in the Coal Mine: Kaufmann Report Warns of 'Academic Freedom in Crisis,'" *FIRE: Newsdesk*, March 8, 2021. Accessed January 8, 2021. https://www.the-fire.org/news/canaries-coal-mine-kaufmann-report-warns-academic-freedom-crisis.

themselves out of public visibility. If they did not, then they could expect harassment and censorship from someone more powerful than they.

For a society to care about free expression, and then cite the analogy of a canary in a coal mine, then the society must care about the canaries, not just the coal companies and their agents patrolling above. As uncomfortable as it may be to realize individuals and organizations applying white supremacy, ableism, and body size discrimination has occurred throughout American history. From racism, anti-fat bias, and discrimination against people with disabilities, these ideas have always enjoyed at least some level of access to the levers of power. To create a truly free society, where free expression is valued then previously marginalized peoples must be allowed the same access to promote their experiences. Anything less is just helping the already powerful a continuation of their monopoly and ignoring those we have too often discriminated against.

As Alessandra Grima said:

> That's what pisses me off the most when I started [posting content], because my aunt was like, "You should cover your arms. People are going to say stuff about you." And I'm like, "I'm an adult, and people have been saying it since I was eleven. How about you shut the fuck up because I was eleven and nobody came to my aid then. But now that I'm an adult, you are trying to police my body? But when I was eleven, it was cool?" ... When I was a waitress at fourteen, nobody was telling the guy not to tell me to sit on his lap ... But now that I'm trying to be comfortable in myself, now it's okay for you to speak up about it. What's that about? What's that about!?!? I think people are more comfortable with pedophilia than my fat body for some reason. Does a woman owning herself scare people more? Apparently, in my experience. That's a weird area to explore. I didn't really realize that until just now ... Oh, wow ... That's a whole can of worms. A lot of inappropriate things happened to me publicly as an underage person that nobody did anything about or said or acknowledged. But when I'm of age and trying to be confident in my body, now they're pissed. That's really ... that could be a whole book. You know what I mean?[11]

---

[11] Alessandra Grima interviewed by Wesley R. Bishop, Providence, Rhode Island, Nov. 21, 2022.

BIBLIOGRAPHY

SECONDARY SOURCES

APAG. "Instagram Policy Team Meets With APAG, Listens to Adult Performers' Concerns." APAG blog, June 21, 2019, accessed January 5, 2023. https://apagunion.com/2019/06/21/instagram-policy-team-meets-with-apag-listens-to-adult-performers-concerns/

Arendt, Hannah. *The Human Condition.* Chicago: University of Chicago Press, 1958.

Banet-Weiser, Sarah. *Empowered: Popular Feminism and Popular Misogyny.* Durham: Duke University Press, 2018.

Benjamin, Ruha. *Race After Technology: Abolitionist Tools for the New Jim Code.* New York: Polity, 2019.

Banet-Weiser, Sarah. *The Most Beautiful Girl in the World: Beauty Pageants and National Identity.* Berkeley: University of California Press, 1999.

Blackwood, Nicole. "Glitter, sequins and liberation." *Chicago Tribune*, July 4, 2019. pp. 4-1-4-4.

Buni, Catherine and Soraya Chemaly. "The Unsafety Net: How Social Media Turned against Women." *Atlantic*, Oct. 9, 2014 Accessed on December 21, 2023. https://www.theatlantic.com/technology/archive/2014/10/the-unsafety-net-how-social-media-turned-against-women/381261/

Cooper, Charlotte. *Fat Activism: A Radical Social Movement.* Bristol, Eng.: HammerOn Press, 2016.

Clark, Nell. "Trump's Social Media Site Hits the App Store a Year after He Was Banned from Twitter." npr.com, Feb. 22, 2022. Accessed January 6, 2024.

© The Author(s), under exclusive license to Springer Nature Switzerland AG 2024
W. R. Bishop, B. N. Rigakos, *Liberating Fat Bodies*,
https://doi.org/10.1007/978-3-031-63890-9

https://www.npr.org/2022/02/22/1082243094/trumps-social-media-app-launches-year-after-twitter-ban

Crawford, Kate, and Tarleton Gillespie. "What Is a Flag for? Social Media Reporting Tools and the Vocabulary of Complaint." *New Media & Society*, 18 (no. 3, 2016), 410–28.

Dickson, E. J. "Why Did Instagram Confuse These Ads Featuring LGBTQ People for Escort Ads?" *Rolling Stone*, July 11, 2019. Accessed January 5, 2024. https://www.rollingstone.com/culture/culture-features/instagram-transgender-sex-workers-857667/

Dremann, Sue. "Nursing Moms Protest Facebook Censorship." Palo Alto Online, Dec. 29, 2008. Accessed January 5, 2023. https://www.paloaltoonline.com/news/2008/12/29/nursing-moms-protest-facebook-censorship

Feinstein, Anthony, Blair Audet, and Elizabeth Waknine. "Witnessing Images of Extreme Violence: A Psychological Study of Journalists in the Newsroom." *JRSM Open* 5 (no. 8, 2014), 1–7.

Fung, Brian and Clare Duffy, "Elon Musk Says He Would Reverse Twitter's Trump Ban." *CNN Business*, May 10, 2022. Accessed September 9, 2023. https://www.cnn.com/2022/05/10/tech/elon-musk-twitter-trump-ban/index.html

Gadarian, Shana. "How Sensationalist TV Stories on Terrorism Make Americans More Hawkish." *Washington Post*, Oct. 9, 2014. Accessed December 21, 2023. https://www.washingtonpost.com/news/monkey-cage/wp/2014/10/09/how-sensationalist-tv-stories-on-terrorism-make-americans-more-hawkish/

Gillespie, Tarleton. *Custodians of the Internet: Platforms, Content Moderation, and the Hidden Decisions That Shape Social Media*. New Haven: Yale University Press, 2021.

Gordon, Aubrey. "How 'Body Positivity' Got Hijacked by Brands and Influencers." *Self*, Jan. 9, 2023a. Accessed December 21, 2023. https://www.self.com/story/aubrey-gordon-book-excerpt

Lo, Tiffany. "'I'm an adult star—trolls call me fat but I'm healthier than people half my size.'" *Daily Star*, July 4, 2023. Accessed January 7, 2024. https://www.dailystar.co.uk/real-life/im-adult-star-trolls-call-30383921

Gordon, Aubrey. *What We Don't Talk about When We Talk about Fat.* Boston: Beacon Press, 2020.

Gordon, Aubrey. *"You Just Need to Lose Weight" And 19 Other Myths About Fat People* Boston: Beacon Press, 2023b.

Grant, Melissa Gira. "The Real Story of the Bipartisan Anti-Sex Trafficking Bill that Failed Miserably on Its Own Terms." *New Republic*, June 23, 2021 Accessed January 7, 2024. https://newrepublic.com/article/162823/sex-trafficking-sex-work-sesta-fosta

Gregg, Melissa. *Counterproductive: Time Management in the Knowledge Economy.* Durham: Duke University Press, 2018.

Gregoire, Carolyn. "What Constant Exposure to Negative News is Doing to Our Mental Health." *HuffPost*, Feb. 19, 2015. Accessed December 21, 2023. https://www.huffpost.com/entry/violent-media-anxiety_n_6671732

Guntarik, Olivia, and Victoria Grieve-Williams, eds. *From Sit-ins to #revolutions: Media and the Changing Nature of Protests.* London: Bloomsbury Publishing, 2020.

Habermas, Jurgen. *The Structural Transformation of the Public Sphere: An Inquiry into a Category of Bourgeois Society.* Trans. Thomas Burger and Frederick Lawrence. Cambridge: MIT Press, 1991.

Hanna, Jon. "We Removed Something You Posted." *Thank You for Swallowing.* June 28, 2016. Accessed December 22, 2023. https://thankyouforswallowing.wordpress.com/2016/06/28/we-removed-something-you-posted/

Harrison, Da'Shaun L. Belly of the Beast: The Politics of Anti-Fatness as Anti-Blackness. San Francisco: North Atlantic Books, 2021.

Icasiano, Spencer. "This Boston Artist Protests Social Media Censors and Celebrates Photographing Nipples." *WBUR.org*, Aug. 2, 2019. Accessed January 5, 2024. https://www.wbur.org/news/2019/08/02/ally-schmaling-instagram-censorship-nipples

Kirkland, Anna. *Fat Rights: Dilemmas of Difference and Personhood.* New York: NYU Press, 2008.

Kosseff, Jeff. *The Twenty-Six Words that Created the Internet.* New York: Cornell University Press, 2019.

Krasinski, Jennifer. "Goings on about Town: Art, Jesse Duquette." *New Yorker*, May 5–June 8, 2023. https://www.newyorker.com/goings-on-about-town/art/jesse-duquette

LeBesco, Kathleen. *Revolting Bodies? The Struggle to Redefine Fat Identity.* Amherst: University of Massachusetts Press, 2003.

Liptak, Adam. "Supreme Court Won't Hold Tech Companies Liable for User Posts." *New York Times,* May 18, 2023. Accessed January 8, 2024. https://www.nytimes.com/2023/05/18/us/politics/supreme-court-google-twitter-230.html?auth=login-google1tap&login=google1tap

Lukianoff, Greg, and Johathan Haidt. *The Coddling of the American Mind: How Good Intentions and Bad Ideas are Setting Up a Generation for Failure.* New York: Penguin Books, 2019.

McRobbie, Angela. *The Aftermath of Feminism: Gender, Culture and Social Change.* Los Angeles: SAGE Publications, 2009.

Milmo, Dan, and Clea Skopeliti. "Teenage girls, body image and Instagram's 'perfect storm.'" In *The Guardian,* Sept. 18, 2021. Accessed February 15, 2023. https://www.theguardian.com/technology/2021/sep/18/teenage-girls-body-image-and-instagrams-perfect-storm

Milosevic, Tijana. *Protecting Children Online?: Cyberbullying Policies of Social Media Companies.* Cambridge: MIT Press, 2018.

Moore, Elaine. "The Truth about 'Shadowbanning' Is More Complicated than Influencers Think." *Financial Times*, March 12, 2022. Accessed January 3, 2023. https://www.ft.com/content/532d7a85-33c8-4488-a57d-9b226c77417a

Mortensen, Torill Elvira. "Anger, Fear, and Games: The Long Event of #GamerGate." *Games and Culture* 13:8 (2018), 787–806.

Mzezewa, Tariro. "What Happened to the Plus-Size Models?" *The Cut*, March 14, 2023. Accessed June 1, 2023. https://www.thecut.com/2023/03/what-happened-to-the-plus-size-models.html

Nakamura, Lisa. *Digitizing Race: Visual Cultures of the Internet*. St. Paul: University of Minnesota Press, 2007.

Nelson, Maggie. *Bluets*. New York: Wave Books, 2009.

O'Neil, Cathy. *Weapons of Math Destruction: How Big Data Increases Inequality and Threatens Democracy*. New York: Crown, 2016.

Perrigo, Billy. "Instagram Makes Teen Girls Hate Themselves. Is that a Bug or Feature?" *Time*, Sept. 16, 2021. Accessed February 15, 2023. https://time.com/6098771/instagram-body-image-teen-girls/

Pfefferkorn, Riana. "The EARN IT Act is Back, and It's More Dangerous than Ever." Stanford Law School, Center for Inter and Society, Feb. 4, 2022. Accessed January 7, 2024. https://cyberlaw.stanford.edu/blog/2022/02/earn-it-act-back-and-it%E2%80%99s-more-dangerous-ever

Phillips, Whitney. *This Is Why We Can't Have Nice Things: Mapping the Relationship Between Online Trolling and Mainstream Culture*. Cambridge: MIT Press, 2016.

Ralston, Meredith. *Slut-Shaming, Whorephobia, and the Unfinished Sexual Revolution*. Toronto: McGill-Queen's University Press, 2021.

Roberts, Sarah T. *Behind the Screen: Content Moderation in the Shadows of Social Media*. New Haven: Yale University Press, 2021.

Romano, Aja. "A New Law Intended to Curb Sex Trafficking Threatens the Future of the Internet as We Know It." Vox.com, July 2, 2018. Accessed January 7, 2024. https://www.vox.com/culture/2018/4/13/17172762/fosta-sesta-backpage-230-internet-freedom

Rosenberg, Yair. "Elon Musk's Latest Target Hits Back." *Atlantic*, Sept. 8, 2023. Accessed September 9, 2023. https://www.theatlantic.com/ideas/archive/2023/09/adl-twitter-jonathan-greenblatt/675258/

Roundtree, Cheyenne, and Laura Bradley. "Only Fans Turns Its Back on Sex Workers and They Are Pissed." *Daily Beast*, Aug. 19, 2021. Accessed December 15, 2022. https://www.thedailybeast.com/onlyfans-turns-its-back-on-sex-workers-and-they-are-pissed

Ruane, Kate. "The EARN It Act is a Disaster for Online Speech and Privacy, Especially for the LGBTQ and Sex Worker Communities." ACLU.org, June 30, 2020. Accessed January 7, 2024. https://www.aclu.org/news/free-speech/the-earn-it-act-is-a-disaster-for-online-speech-and-privacy-especially-for-the-lgbtq-and-sex-worker-communities

Saraswati, L. Ayu. *Pain Generation: Social Media, Feminist Activism, and the Neoliberal Selfie*. New York: NYU Press, 2021.

Sennett, Richard. *The Fall of Public Man*. New York: W.W. Norton & Company, 1976.

Shapiro, Emma. "Free the Nipple: A History of a Hidden Movement." *Hyperallergic*, Oct. 5, 2021. Accessed January 5, 2023. https://hyperallergic.com/681937/free-the-nipple-a-history-of-a-hidden-movement/

Spangler, Todd. "Instagram CEO Positions His Company as Safer Alternative to Controversial Rivals." *Variety*, Nov. 15, 2017. Accessed February 13, 2023. https://variety.com/2017/digital/features/instagram-ceo-kevin-systrom-1202614763/

Stevens, Sean. "Canaries in the Coal Mine: Kaufmann Report Warns of 'Academic Freedom in Crisis.'" *FIRE: Newsdesk*, March 8, 2021. Accessed January 8, 2021. https://www.thefire.org/news/canaries-coal-mine-kaufmann-report-warns-academic-freedom-crisis

Strings, Sabrina. *Fearing the Black Body: The Racial Origins of Fat Phobia*. New York: NYU Press, 2019.

Sullivan, Margaret. "Elon Musk's Hypocrisy about Free Speech Hits New Low." *Guardian*, Sept. 7, 2023. Accessed September 9, 2023. https://www.theguardian.com/commentisfree/2023/sep/07/elon-musks-hypocrisy-about-free-speech-hits-a-new-low

Swami, Viren. "Why the Body Positivity Movement Risks Turning Toxic." *The Conversation*, Sept. 14, 2022. Accessed, December 21, 2023. https://theconversation.com/why-the-body-positivity-movement-risks-turning-toxic-189913

Taylor, Sonya Renee. *The Body Is Not an Apology: The Power of Radical Self-Love*. Los Angeles: Berrett-Koehler Publishers, 2018.

The Learning Network. "What Students Are Saying about How Social Media Affects Their Body Image." *New York Times*, March 31, 2022. Accessed February 15, 2023. https://www.nytimes.com/2022/03/31/learning/what-students-are-saying-about-how-social-media-affects-their-body-image.html

Tripp, Heidi. "All Sex Workers Deserve Protection: How FOSTA/SESTA Overlooks Consensual Sex Workers in an Attempt to Protect Sex Trafficking Victims." *Penn State Law Review*, 124 (no. 1, 2019). Accessed January 12, 2024 https://elibrary.law.psu.edu/pslr/vol124/iss1/6

Tolentino, Jia. *Trick Mirror: Reflections on Self-delusion*. New York: Random House, 2020.

Tolman, Deborah L. *Dilemmas of Desire: Teenage Girls Talk about Sexuality*. Cambridge: Harvard University Press, 2002.

Tsoulis-Reay, Alexa. *Finding Normal: Sex, Love, and Taboo in Our Hyperconnected World.* New York: St. Martin's Press, 2021.

Tufekci, Zeynep. *Twitter and Tear Gas: The Power and Fragility of Networked Protest.* New Haven: Yale University Press, 2018.

West, Lindy. *Shrill: Notes from a Loud Woman.* New York: Hachette Books, 2016.

INTERVIEWS

Jackie Barthelemy interview by Wesley R. Bishop, Chicago, Illinois, Nov. 4, 2019.

Phaedra Black interview by Wesley R. Bishop, Chicago, Illinois, Nov. 4, 2019.

Annie Brown Zoom interview by Wesley R. Bishop, Sept. 29, 2021.

Dimple Dutchess interview by Wesley R. Bishop, Chicago, Illinois, Nov. 4, 2019.

Val Elefante Zoom interview by Wesley R. Bishop, Sept. 9, 2021.

Alessandra Grima Zoom interview by Wesley R. Bishop, April 4, 2022.

Alessandra Grima interview by Wesley R. Bishop, Providence, Rhode Island, Nov. 21, 2022.

Audrey Grison. "Interview with Audrey Grison: Disability, Art, and the Self." By Wesley R. Bishop. *North Meridian Review,* 4 (Fall 2023), 136–52.

Grey Johnson Zoom interview by Wesley R. Bishop, May 27, 2022.

Asstyn Martin Zoom interview by Wesley R. Bishop, June 24, 2021.

Jessie Oliver interview by Wesley R. Bishop, Chicago, Illinois, Nov. 4, 2019.

Vivienne Rose interview by Wesley R. Bishop, Indianapolis, Indiana, May 20, 2021.

Rose, Vivienne. "Myths Concerning Fatness and Body Size." Roundtable with Wesely R. Bishop at annual *Southern Humanities Council.* Holiday Inn Riverwalk Hotel, San Antonio, Texas, Jan. 27, 2023.

Shero, Carina. "Instagram Deleted Her Account @ Over 400K Followers: Fat Phobia in Art and Social Media, and How Carina Shero Continues to Fight for Better Representation of All Bodies." By Wesley R. Bishop, *TERSE.* April 15, 2018. https://tersejournal.com/2018/04/19/instagram-deleted-her-account-over-400k-followers-fat-phobia-in-art-and-social-media-and-how-carina-shero-continues-to-fight-for-better-representation-of-all-bodies/

Carina Shero interview by Wesley R. Bishop, Chicago, Illinois, Nov. 4, 2019.

Carina Shero, interview by Wesley R. Bishop, Chicago, Illinois, April 14, 2022.

Robina Strowder interview by Wesley R. Bishop, Chicago, Illinois, Nov. 4, 2019.

Essence Walker interview by Wesley R. Bishop, Chicago, Illinois, Nov. 4, 2019.

Saucye West interview by Wesley R. Bishop, via Zoom call, Aug. 9, 2021.

Danielle Whitfield interview by Wesley R. Bishop, Chicago, Illinois, Nov. 4, 2019.

Laura Weetzie Wilson interview by Wesley R. Bishop, Chicago, Illinois, Nov. 4, 2019.

INDEX[1]

[1] Note: Page numbers followed by 'n' refer to notes.

GPSR Compliance

The European Union's (EU) General Product Safety Regulation (GPSR) is a set of rules that requires consumer products to be safe and our obligations to ensure this.

If you have any concerns about our products, you can contact us on ProductSafety@springernature.com

In case Publisher is established outside the EU, the EU authorized representative is:

Springer Nature Customer Service Center GmbH
Europaplatz 3
69115 Heidelberg, Germany

The manufacturer's authorised representative in the EU is Springer
Nature Customer Service Centre GmbH, Europaplatz 3, 69115 Heidelberg,
Germany. If you have any concerns regarding our products, please
contact ProductSafety@springernature.com

Printed and bound by CPI Group (UK) Ltd, Croydon, CR0 4YY
27/04/2026
02097563-0016